Creative Seed Bead CONNECTIONS

Using Wire, Jump Rings, and Chain

Teresa Meister

KB
KALMBACH BOOKS

Step-by-step photography by Jason Meister. All other photography © 2013 Kalmbach Books.

Published in 2013

17 16 15 14 13   1 2 3 4 5

Manufactured in the United States of America

ISBN: 978-0-87116-479-7
EISBN: 978-0-87116-779-8

Editor: Mary Wohlgemuth
Art Director: Lisa Bergman
Technical Editor: Jane Danley Cruz
Associate Editor: Erica Swanson
Layout Designer: Lisa Schroeder
Photographers: James Forbes, William Zuback
Illustrator: Teresa Meister

Library of Congress Cataloging in Publication Data

Meister, Teresa.
    Creative seed bead connections : using wire, jump rings, and chain / Teresa Meister.

        p. : col. ill. ; cm.

    Issued also as an ebook.
    ISBN: 978-0-87116-479-7

    1. Beadwork—Patterns. 2. Beadwork—Handbooks, manuals, etc. 3. Jewelry making—Handbooks, manuals, etc. I. Title. II. Title: Seed bead connections

TT860 .M45 2013
745.594/2

Contents

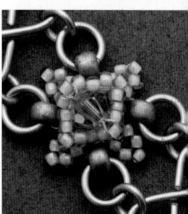

I felt a powerful connection when I laid my eyes on a rainbow-filled wall of seed beads more than 20 years ago.

Making Connections

This book is a tangible point along my creative journey, and I am thrilled to share it with you.

My creative journey began with the tiny and oh-so-magical seed bead. I felt a powerful connection when I laid my eyes on a rainbow-filled wall of seed beads in a craft store more than 20 years ago. The more I played with these tiny glass gems, the closer I came to connecting with my own imagination. For years I worked in isolation, admiring other artists' work and learning traditional stitches through books. But something was still missing. It wasn't until I joined a weekly gathering of seed beaders at my local bead store that my creativity started to blossom. It was a revelation to me that sharing skills, ideas, successes, and failures with other people is what fuels the creative journey and what makes it so extraordinary. By broadening my world to embrace personal connections, I found the courage to let go of fear, to be creatively adventurous, and to create authentically.

These personal connections are what powered me forward and have led me here. I had no idea when I met my friend Chrisa several years ago that our connection would lead me to write this book. Our friendship began when we discovered we shared a passion for jewelry making. We also found out where our interests differed: I love beadweaving and she loves wireworking. Over time, we experimented with each other's medium and enthusiastically shared our individual expertise. As I added jump rings, wire, and chain to my beloved seed beads, I found what made my heart sing, and new designs started to surface. Mixing off-loom beadweaving with wireworking opened up a new world of creative possibilities to me. This book shares this new design direction.

My ultimate desire is to make a meaningful connection with you through this book and inspire you to reach out and do the same through your work. It is the ever-expanding circle of connections that inspires our creative souls. Open up to the creative possibilities of making new connections and the adventure of what will be. It all starts with fearless discovery.

Teresa

How to Use This Book

THE PROJECTS

These projects are designed to introduce beadweavers to simple wireworking techniques. As a beadweaver, you likely have experience with making stitched components, so I ordered the projects to build your wireworking skills.

Project section 1: *Beginning* with the most basic techniques used throughout the projects, this section presents techniques for working with jump rings and chain. You'll also learn how to coil wire.

Project section 2: *Broadening* your experience, this section combines the skills learned in the first section with techniques for making eyepins, wrapped loops, and simple wire shapes.

Project section 3: *Building* on the skills established in the first two chapters, the final chapter presents designs that incorporate beads directly into wire shapes.

The nature of the projects makes it easy to adjust the length of any of the accessories; simply add or subtract stitched components or wire links. You can also lengthen or shorten the pieces of chain on the ends of some necklaces.

INSTRUCTION FORMAT

All but one of the projects is composed of a set of three jewelry accessories: a bracelet, a necklace, and a pair of earrings. (One project in the final section, Give It a Swirl, features a ring in place of earrings.)

You'll find instructions for the jewelry piece you want to make under the heading "Accessories." These steps will refer you to the preceding beadweaving or wirework instructions for making individual components. Look for additional information and final assembly instructions under the specific accessory.

ILLUSTRATIONS AND PHOTOS

Illustrations designated by a figure number supplement the step-by-step beadweaving and accessory assembly instructions.

Beadweaving figures: When multiple thread paths are shown in a single figure, they will be shown in various colors, always ending in black. Each new color starts with a dot. A black star indicates the end of a thread. A dotted line indicates the thread is passing through a bead. Beads picked up in the current step are fully saturated with color. If a bead is shown in lighter, less-saturated color, it was added in a previous step.

In some cases, for reasons of space and repetition, the figure doesn't show the entire accessory. Wavy lines as pictured below indicate that part of a pattern is not shown.

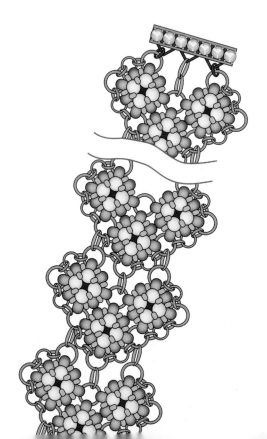

Assembly figures: In the majority of assembly figures, the size of the jump ring is indicated by color. Ranging from the smallest to the largest, the colors and sizes are: dark green for ³⁄₃₂ in., bright blue for ⅛ in., and yellow for ³⁄₁₆ in. The actual wire color is used when the size of the jump ring is obvious. When it is not as obvious, the jump rings or chain added in previous steps are represented in a less-saturated color. For example, the Out of Idleness assembly figure for the pendant and earrings use this convention.

Photographs: Processes for working with jump rings, wire, and chain are shown in photographs. Photos are used in the "Basic Techniques: Wirework" section and the Wirework sections of individual projects.

MY DESIGN PROCESS

For me, the design process is about seeing something new, sharing what I see with other people, and then looking for something new again.

The similarities and the variations among the projects' stitched components offer some insight into my way of seeing something new. This can happen when I am looking and when I am not.

When I am looking, I consciously ask myself, "How can I manipulate this component to create something new?" Often I see something new when I am not trying to see and my mind is quiet. The creative process is an infinite cycle of evolution and revolution—as long as you are open to seeing and sharing it.

Materials

colored polyethylene thread

Beadweaving Materials

BEADING THREAD

The majority of the projects in the book use pearls or crystals, and all of the projects incorporate wire that comes in direct contact with beads. Because these materials can abrade and cut standard beading thread quite easily, I recommend using Fireline or another type of polyethylene thread to make the projects in the book. Fireline 6 lb. test works well; this thread is sturdy yet thin, it doesn't tear on the sharp edges of crystals, and at just 0.15mm thick, it can pass several times through 15° seed beads. I recently discovered a supplier who offers Fireline in many colors applied after manufacture; for some components and stitches where a lot of thread shows, choose a color that coordinates with your beads.

seed beads

BEADS

I use a mixture of different types and sizes of beads to shape the stitched components in the book. Many of you are already familiar with the categories of beads that follow, so rather than go into great detail about each bead's properties, I'll point out some of my preferences.

Seed beads
To me, these are little gems made of glass. They are the foundation of my designs —the material and means from which I build each creation. An abundance of colors, shapes, cuts, finishes, and sizes are available from several manufacturers. Size is indicated by the ° symbol with a number in front of it; the higher the number, the smaller the bead. I prefer round Japanese-made seed beads in sizes 15° and 8° and use these in combination in almost all the projects in the book.

Be on the lookout for any bead that is irregularly shaped or has a narrow hole, and discard it. A misshapen bead can skew a design: The beadwork just won't sit right as subsequent beads are added. When a bead has a narrow hole, multiple thread passes through the bead may become a problem, and too many passes will break the bead.

All of the projects use 8° beads as connection points for the wire components in the design; a wire link or a jump ring is threaded through the bead. If the 8° is misshapen or its hole is too narrow, the wire may not pass through, so please pay special attention when choosing an 8° to stitch into a component.

Drops
Manufactured by Miyuki, these tiny, 3.4mm raindrop-shaped beads have a hole through the top of the drop. Part of their charm is each bead's uniqueness; you'll notice quite a range in shape, and the holes are not uniformly sized. You may need to try several drops before you find one with an opening large enough for the wire or jump ring to fit through.

drops

crystals

pearls

Czech glass

Crystals

Sometimes a piece comes alive with just a little sparkle. Sometimes it calls for full-blown bling. Crystals answer both calls. Like seed beads, crystals are available from a choice of manufacturers and come in lots of colors, shapes, cuts, finishes, and sizes. I frequently turn to 3mm and 4mm bicone crystals as an integral design element and use a crystal pendant for the perfect finishing touch. I used both Swarovski and Preciosa crystals for the projects, choosing based on the color, shape, size, and level of sparkle most suited to the jewelry piece.

Pearls

I use both synthetic and freshwater pearls in my designs. Synthetic pearls, also known as imitation or faux pearls, are manufactured around a core of glass, crystal, ceramic, shell, or plastic. The core is coated to simulate the look and sometimes the feel of the real thing. I used Swarovski crystal pearls in these designs because of their uniform quality, durability, and ability to closely mimic the luster and weight of natural pearls.

Freshwater pearls are developed by making a small cut into the tissue of a young shellfish called a mollusk and inserting a small piece of mantle from a donor mollusk. The result is a deposit of almost pure nacre, and *viola!*—a pearl. Freshwater pearls come in a variety of colors. Color may be produced naturally or from dyeing, bleaching, chemically altering, or irradiating.

Czech glass

At bead shows, I love digging through tables piled high with hanks of assorted glass beads made in the Czech Republic. The assortment includes basic and novelty shapes. Some of my picks—basic 4x6mm teardrops, fire-polished drops, and novelty glass leaves, for example— have emerged in the projects in this book. Other picks wait to be made into designs, but then again, other beads wait to be picked. I can't wait to dig in at the next bead show!

Spacers

Used to accent focal beads and provide breathing room in jewelry design, these beads have relatively large holes, so they can be strung on a variety of materials.

spacers

Materials

chain

Wirework Materials

CHAIN

Jewelry chain is available in a huge variety of metals, link sizes, and styles. I use it as a unifying decorative element in many of my designs. Often I use good-quality plated metal (rather than solid metal or metal-filled chain). When buying plated chain, I determine the quality by checking that the links are solidly connected and the chain has no sharp edges or discoloration.

Plated chain is economical (I must admit it pains me a little when I cut sterling silver or 14k gold chain into the pieces called for in the project instructions. Oh, those tiny discarded links!). It comes in a variety of colors, including an antique finish I especially like. For the projects that use chain, the materials list includes 20% more than the actual length of chain needed to complete the accessory. The extra inches give you some wiggle room and some peace of mind.

open jump rings

closed jump rings

JUMP RINGS

Open jump rings

An open jump ring has a perfect flush cut so it can be opened and closed. Rather than make my own jump rings, which is a lot of work and can be imprecise, I buy jump rings manufactured for making chain mail jewelry. Chain mail is made by connecting metal rings in a pattern that relies on uniformity in ring sizes. Some projects in the book call for this consistency. Not all jump ring makers follow the method described below and, as a result, you have to be careful when purchasing jump rings; contact the supplier if you need more information.

The jump rings used for the projects in the book are measured by the *inside diameter* (ID) of the ring and are true to size. As mentioned earlier, I use three sizes of open jump rings: 3/32 in., 1/8 in., and 3/16 in.

The true size of a jump ring depends on the specific type of metal wire used, its gauge (diameter), and its temper (degree of hardness), as well as the size of the mandrel used to make the jump ring.

As an example, copper is a soft metal and has very little *spring-back*, which refers to the degree the wire will resist being coiled and its tendency to spring back to its original shape. Aluminum is harder and has more spring-back. Copper and aluminum jump rings coiled on the same mandrel would be two different sizes. The manufacturers I use account for these differences in metal properties; look for the "true to size" designation if the project you're making requires precise sizes of jump rings.

Like the practice of buying a sufficient quantity of the beads from a single dye lot to compete a design, I recommend that you purchase an adequate quantity of jump rings in a single purchase to complete a project. This will prevent undesirable results due to a variation in manufacturing.

Closed jump rings

These jump rings are soldered to form a continuous ring. They ensure an extra-secure closure.

WIRE

Wire is an essential material on my supply list. Some properties of wire were described in the information about jump rings. Here is more detail about wire.

Shape

Look at a cut end of a piece of wire to see its profile or shape. Wire is sold in several profiles, including half-round, square, and—the most common—round, which is the only shape used for the projects in this book.

Temper

Temper refers to a wire's hardness or softness. In manufacturing, different degrees of temper are achieved according to the number of times the wire is pulled through a draw plate. Referred to as work-hardening, the more draws the harder the wire becomes. The hardest temper is called *spring-hard*; spring-hard wire will tend to spring back to its original shape. *Half-hard* wire is often used to construct a wire bezel around a cabochon.

All the projects in the book call for *dead-soft* wire. This temper is ideal for creating links and clasps because the wire is pliable, yet the resulting shapes hold up well when coupled with the stitched components because the components are quite lightweight. Because of its softness, this wire is at a higher risk for being marred as you work it. You'll find my recommendations for some specific wirework tools (described in the Tools section) that reduce this risk.

Gauge

Gauge refers to a wire's thickness or diameter. The higher the wire's gauge number, the thinner the wire. All of the projects in the book use 20- or 24-gauge wire; I use 20-gauge to shape decorative wire links and eyepin links, and 24-gauge to make wrapped-loop links.

Types

I use a variety of wire types including precious metal, base metal, and permanently colored copper wire for the designs in the book. The precious metal I use most frequently is sterling silver. It remains affordable compared with gold-filled wire. Another alternative to gold-filled wire is red brass wire, which is an alloy of 70% copper and 30% zinc and has a pleasingly warm golden tone. In several projects, I use nontarnish copper wire, which has a special finish to help protect it from discoloring. I use two colors of permanently colored copper wire made by Parawire: bronze and titanium. The bronze has a luminous orange glow, and the titanium color is applied over silver-plated copper, creating an attractive antique-silver tone.

> **▶TIP** Although none of my project instructions call for work-hardening or texturing wire, I recommend that you never hammer colored wire; the colored surface may chip away.

20-gauge wire (left) and 24-gauge

colored copper-based wire

Materials

headpins

HEADPINS

Made from wire, headpins come in varying lengths from ½ in. to 4 in. The pin has a plain or decorative cap at one end to keep the bead(s) from falling off. When headpins are used in jewelry making, the end opposite the cap is often finished with a wrapped loop.

Other Materials

ARTISAN-DESIGNED COMPONENTS

Artisan-designed beads, spacers, clasps, chandeliers, connectors, links, and pendants provide an immense source of inspiration for my designs. It's as though a little bolt of creative energy flows through me when I connect with an artist's work, and that artist's vision is shared with mine when the connection creatively transforms into a new design.

CLASPS

Choosing a clasp an important design decision. Clasps are an integral part of every necklace and bracelet design. Choose among toggle, tube, box, magnetic, lobster claw, spring ring, and hook-and-eye clasps. You can even learn how to make your own following the instructions in several projects.

artisan-designed components

BAILS

Jewelry bails allow a pendant to hang from a neck chain or strap. Bails are often distinguished by their attachment method. To hang stitched components, I sometimes use a pinch or prong bail, which has prongs on the inside that grasp the beadwork.

EARRING FINDINGS

I use French hook findings for my earring designs. This shape has a clean, elegant look and feel. I recommend securing it with a rubber or plastic clutch.

JEWELRY CARE

Over time, contact with air will tarnish precious and base metals. Since the jewelry pieces you'll be making are mixture of metals and stitched components, you shouldn't dip or soak them in any type of liquid polishing solution. If the wire discolors, use a jewelry polishing cloth to remove the tarnish from the metal. Use a soft brush to remove dust or debris. Store the jewelry in a plastic bag to limit its exposure to the elements.

earring wires

bail

clasps

Tools

Beadweaving Tools

NEEDLES

I use size #12 Pony beading needles for most of my beadwork and for all of the projects. Certain bead arrangements and thread paths in some of the stitched components are a little rough on my needles. Over time, needles bend, and I find that the eye of the needle can narrow as well. This narrowing can abrade the thread as I stitch, causing it to break where it passes through the eye, so I always have plenty of needles on hand and change out as needed. A worn needle makes a handy tool: Slip an old, bent needle in the hole of an 8° to open up space for a connecting jump ring.

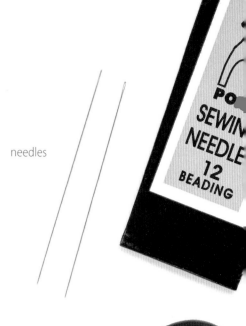

needles

SCISSORS

When I started to use a lot of braided thread, I bought high-durability scissors specifically designed to cut it. Although you don't have to use specialty scissors, the blades have a fine serrated edge that make a nice, even cut.

THREAD BURNER

One of my essential tools, a thread burner is a battery-operated device that literally takes care of loose ends. I use it faithfully every time I start or end a thread to eliminate any evidence of a tail by melting it away. Although the heating element at the tip allows you to precisely target the thread you want to eliminate, use caution so you don't burn through other threads that are integral to your beadwork.

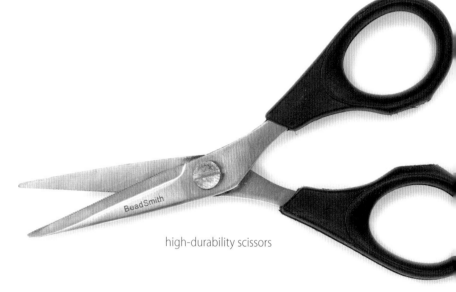

high-durability scissors

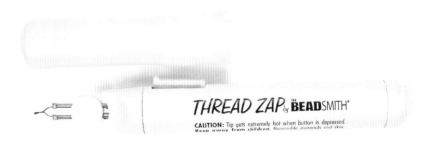

thread burner

Tools

bead scoop

plastic bobbin

BEAD SCOOP

Use this handy little shovel or an empty plastic bead tube to pick up beads from your work surface.

PLASTIC BOBBINS

I was introduced to these bobbins many years ago at my local bead store. Advertised for use in kumihimo and macramé, these are great for storing works in progress. The bobbin is flexible. Flip one curved side up to open it, and wind the working thread around the core to keep the thread from tangling. If I have a small stitched component, I tuck the entire piece in the bobbin and close it. The bobbins are lightweight and stackable, so you can keep several pieces together.

THREAD PULLER

Since I always had a pair of small chainnose pliers handy for wirework while making the projects for this book, I found myself using those to grasp and pull the tiniest tip of stubborn thread through the eye of a needle.

MACARONI NEEDLE PULLER

When the needle needs to be coaxed through a bead, I turn to my Macaroni Needle Puller. This ingenious tool, developed by Sharon Rawson, was named for its small, flexible piece of tubing that resembles a type of pasta. The tubing is placed around the needle for a secure grip. I often reflexively hold my breath as I pull the needle through the bead, but I don't think it makes the needle any slimmer!

WORK SURFACE

Although I have a studio that houses a room full of beads, I am most comfortable beading while sitting on my living room couch. I sit nestled with a pillow behind my back and another on my lap for height and stability, with my velvety-surface beading board on top of the stack. Assorted beads in small piles are sprinkled across the board, and a few needles are poked into a padded corner. My other essential beading supplies are easily accessible on the table next to me, all clearly lit by a daylight floor lamp. My bead board suits how I work. I like that it is portable, because I bead during long car trips (of course, only when I am not driving!). I always have more than one project in progress, so I keep several boards filled with beads and components. The boards can be stacked, beads and all, and quickly moved out of sight.

macaroni needle puller

bentnose pliers

Wirework Tools

CHOOSING WIREWORK TOOLS

Always use wirework tools designed for jewelry making. Don't grab the tools from the home-repair toolkit—they will mar your precious creations. As with most other tools, you'll find a wide range of jewelry tools from which to choose, geared to the beginner, the professional, and anyone in between. You don't need the most expensive and most ergonomic tools, but you will need the tools listed below (or a comparable substitute) to complete all the projects. I've included some of my preferences and recommended uses.

JEWELRY PLIERS

Bentnose pliers

Bentnose pliers have tapered jaws with a slight angle at the tips that makes them invaluable for getting into hard-to-reach places. I use these pliers along with chainnose pliers to close a jump ring when it's threaded through multiple beads and I have only a small amount of wire to grasp.

Chainnose pliers

Chainnose pliers have flat jaws that gradually taper toward the tip. I have several pairs of these, ranging from 4½–6½ in. from the tip of the jaws to the end of the handles. I tend to use the longer pair for opening and closing jump rings if the jump ring is not threaded through more than one bead, which limits the room I have to work with. When making a wire swirl, I use the larger pair because they provide a good grip on the wire as I bend it.

Split-ring pliers

Split-ring pliers have a special bent tip that can be inserted between split rings to open them.

Flush cutters

This tool is used for cutting wire when a flat (or flush) end is needed. I suggest you spend the money for high-quality cutters because a precision cut is essential to high-quality wirework and the cutters' sharpness will last.

Nylon-jaw pliers

Nylon-jaw pliers have wide jaws made of thick nylon, which allow you to straighten wire without marring the finish. Don't go for the least expensive, or they may end up damaging the wire instead of protecting it.

chainnose pliers

split-ring pliers

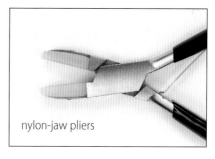
flush cutters

nylon-jaw pliers

Tools

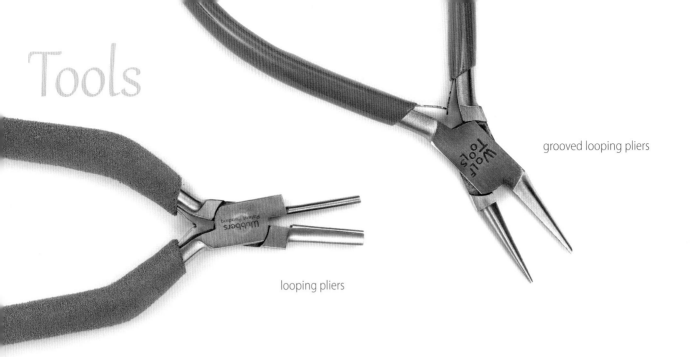

grooved looping pliers

looping pliers

Looping pliers

Having only intermittent success in the past using standard roundnose pliers to make eyepins and wrapped loops, I was pleased when I learned about this specialized tool made by Wubbers. Designed to make it easier to consistently make identical eyepins and wrapped loops, the pliers allow you to make consistent loops with a 2.2mm inside diameter (ID). One jaw is completely round to help prevent marring the wire. The other jaw is concave to match the rounded jaw. This design enables a secure grip on the wire as it engineers the roundness of the loop. You can substitute standard roundnose pliers or a set of stepped pliers to get a close approximation to the 2.2mm desired loop size.

Grooved looping pliers

I love tools that are designed to make the job easier yet give the results I'm after. The grooved looping pliers made by Wolf have one tapered conical jaw and one tapered flat jaw. The flat jaw has grooves at three key points along the taper. These grooves help position and hold wire securely so you can repeat three identical sizes of loops: approximately 2mm, 3mm, and 4mm (ID).

I use these pliers to form many different types of wire links. Because I don't have to worry about the wire slipping from between the jaws and I don't have to mark the pliers to repeat loop sizes, I avoid damaging the wire as I work it. You can substitute standard roundnose pliers (mark the jaws at commonly used points) or a set of stepped pliers that function in the same way.

OTHER TOOLS

Pliers stand

A lightweight wood rack keeps my assortment of wireworking tools neatly organized and handy.

Knitting needles and Sharpie marker

I use these items as mandrels by wrapping wire around them. Choose your mandrel based on the size of curve or coil you want to create. Other cylindrical items such as wood dowels make good mandrels too.

Foldable ruler

This ruler is lightweight, compact, and portable, and it provides measurements in inches and centimeters. I recommend using a 12-in. foldable, plastic ruler to measure wire. A benefit of using this ruler for wirework is that the grooves at each inch mark provide a small channel for flush cutters to fit in when I cut the wire.

mandrels

foldable ruler

Techniques

Beadweaving Techniques
WORKING WITH THREAD

Thread length

The project instructions suggest an approximate length of thread for beginning each stitched component. This recommendation was a comfortable length for me and, in most cases, will allow you to complete a stitched component or series of steps to the point where the instructions direct you to end the thread. Use the thread length that is most comfortable for you.

Adding and ending thread

To add thread, sew into the beadwork several beads prior to the point where the last bead was added, leaving a short tail. If a large bead such as an 8º is available, pass through it and tie a half-hitch knot. Follow the thread path of the stitch and exit the point where the last stitch ended.

To end the thread, sew back through several beads following the thread path of the stitch. If a large bead such as an 8º is available, pass through it and tie a half-hitch knot. Sew through a few more beads and tie a second half-hitch knot. Sew through a few more beads and trim the thread.

Half-hitch knot

Pass the needle under the thread bridge between two beads. Pull gently until a loop forms. Cross back over the thread between the beads, sew through the loop, and pull gently to draw the knot into the beadwork.

Reinforcing a thread path

In some of the projects, the instructions direct you to strengthen the stitched components by passing through the same sequence of beads more than once. This additional support helps pull the beads tight to the component.

Step up

A step-up is used to transition from one round to the next. To step up, sew through the first bead added in the current round.

▶**TIP** All the designs use 8º seed beads as connection points for the wire components, so many 8ºs either have a wire link or a jump ring threaded through the bead. If the 8º is misshapen or its hole is too narrow, the wire may not fit, so it's a good idea to cull your 8ºs before you start stitching.

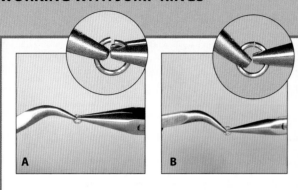

Opening and closing a jump ring

Using two pairs of chainnose or bentnose pliers (or one of each), grasp each end of the jump ring. To prevent the ring from distorting, move one jaw toward you and the other in the opposite direction **[A]**. To close, perform the reverse of the motion used to open the jump ring, but move slightly past the point where the two ends meet. The jump ring will snap back ever so slightly as the two sides meet. This results in a tight, flush connection **[B]**.

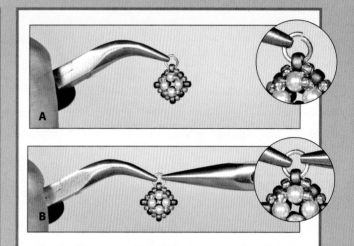

Attaching a jump ring to an 8º in a beaded component

Open a jump ring. Using bentnose pliers, guide the jump ring through the 8º on the beaded component **[A]**. Close the jump ring **[B]**.

Attaching a jump ring to two 8ºs in two beaded components

Open a jump ring. Using bentnose pliers, guide the jump ring through the two desired 8ºs in the two beaded components. Using bentnose pliers and chainnose pliers, grasp either end of the open jump ring. Gently press the jaws of one pliers against the neighboring bead to hold the beads in place. Close the jump ring.

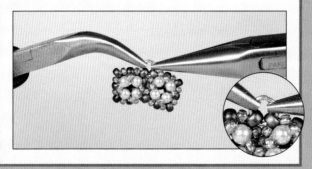

Attaching a jump ring to three 8ºs in three beaded components

Open a jump ring. Using bentnose pliers, guide the jump ring through the three desired 8ºs in the three beaded components. Using bentnose pliers and chainnose pliers, grasp either end of the open jump ring. Gently press the jaws of one set of pliers against the neighboring bead to hold the beads in place. Close the jump ring.

Joining jump rings attached to two beaded components

Open a new jump ring. Pick up the desired jump ring attached to each component. Close the jump ring.

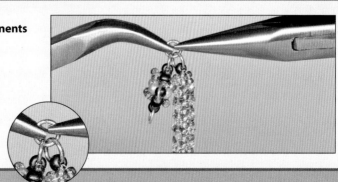

Techniques

Wirework Techniques
WORKING WITH WIRE

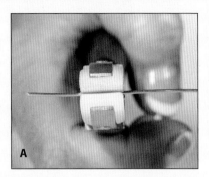

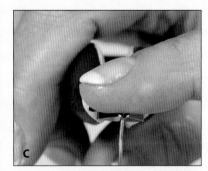

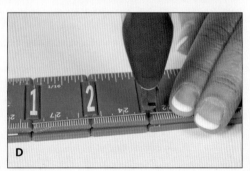

Preparing and flush-cutting wire

To straighten a length of wire, pull it through the jaws of nylon-jaw pliers several times **[A]**. Place one end of the wire between the flush cutters' jaws with the angled side of the jaws up **[B]**. Place your forefinger over the wire to prevent the wire end from shooting into the air, and flush-cut the end **[C]**. Working on the other end, measure and mark the desired length **[D]**. Flush-cut the end. Remember that the flat side of the flush cutters' jaws should face the wire end you are flush-cutting.

Making a P-shaped loop with grooved looping pliers

Prepare the desired length of 20-gauge wire. Position one end of the wire in the desired groove of the looping pliers **[A]**. Roll the hand holding the pliers toward you while bracing the other end of the wire with the forefinger of the other hand to create a P-shaped loop.

Reposition the pliers slightly back and continue to roll forward until the loop touches the straight wire **[B]**.

This technique works with other looping pliers and roundnose pliers as well.

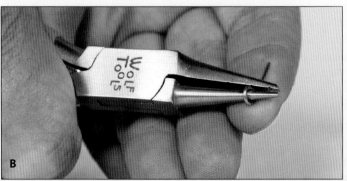

Making a wrapped loop with looping pliers

1 Cut the desired length of 24-gauge wire. Position the wire in the jaws of the looping pliers so a 1-in. length of wire extends from the end **[A]**.

2 Squeeze that jaws, creating an angle that is slightly less than 90 degrees **[B]**. Pull the long wire slightly back and down **[C]**.

3 Bend the short wire so it almost touches the long one **[D]**. Move the pliers slightly forward to reposition the jaws in the loop. Cross the short wire over the long one, forming a 90-degree angle **[E]**. Remove the loop from the pliers.

4 Hold the loop with bentnose or chainnose pliers to keep its shape and use your fingers or another pair of pliers to tightly pull and wrap the short wire around the long wire approximately 2½ times **[F]**. Flush-cut the short end.

5 String the desired bead(s) on the wire. Hold the wire by the loop so the side of the loop is facing you. (Similarly, if you're making a loop on a headpin, hold the endcap.) Position the looping pliers above the bead and squeeze the jaws, creating an almost 90-degree angle in the wire **[G]**. Roll the pliers back to form the neck, and bend the wire down so it almost touches the bead **[H]**.

6 Reposition the jaws slightly forward to leave enough room to bring the wire under the jaw and wrap the wire. Use your fingers or another pair of pliers to bring the wire tightly under the jaw **[I]**. Remove the loop from the pliers.

7 Hold the loop with bentnose or chainnose pliers, and use your fingers or another pair of pliers to tightly pull and wrap the wire around the neck, filling in the space above the bead **[J]**. Flush-cut the wire end.

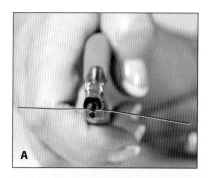

A

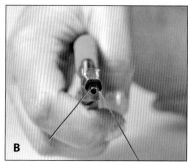

B

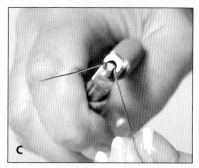

C

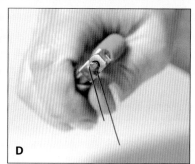

D

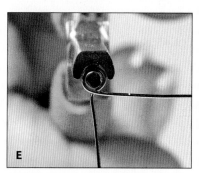

E

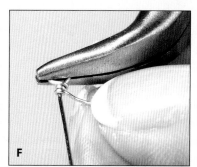

F

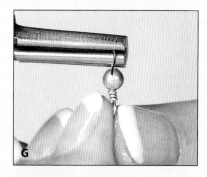

G

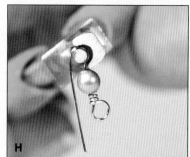

H

I

J

Techniques

WORKING WITH CHAIN

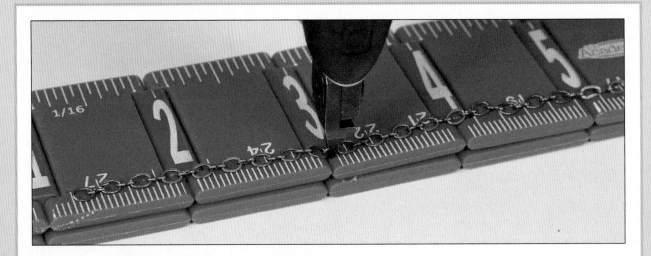

Measuring and cutting chain

When using the chain style specified in a project, count the number of links specified for the accessory you are making. If you are using a different style of chain, stretch the chain against a ruler to reach the measurement indicated for the accessory you are making, and count the number of links needed. The exact measured length may not be precise, but by counting the number of links, the chain length will be the most accurate and consistent. Use flush cutters to cut the next link in the chain to detach the piece.

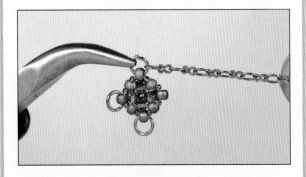

Attaching chain to a jump ring in a beaded component

After threading a jump ring into an 8º seed bead in the beaded component, hold one end of the open jump ring with bentnose pliers, and thread an end link of chain on the jump ring. Close the jump ring.

Attaching a bead to a length of chain

Thread a bead onto an open jump ring, hold one end of the jump ring with bentnose pliers, and thread the desired chain link on the jump ring. Close the jump ring.

Beginning

Weaving beads with needle and thread is the foundation of all the projects. This first group of projects introduces you to the techniques other than beadweaving used throughout this book: working with jump rings and chain, and shaping wire.

Rhythm and Blue Pearl

This set makes me happy. It is the kind of happiness that I feel when I am listening to a song that literally moves me. Before I realize it, I'm absorbed in the music and the moment, moving and singing along. This set is that feeling: a happy rhythm of beads and wire.

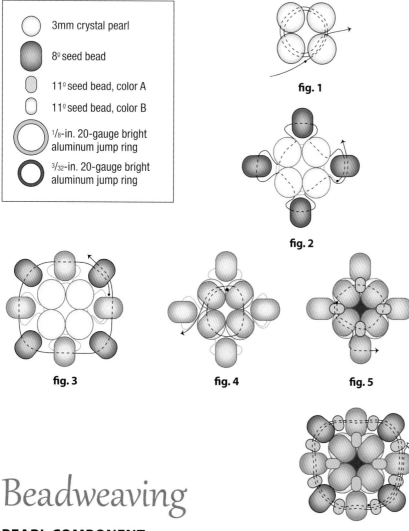

fig. 1

fig. 2

fig. 3   **fig. 4**   **fig. 5**

fig. 6

Beadweaving

PEARL COMPONENT

Single-Sided

1 Round 1: Thread a needle onto 24 in. of thread, pick up four 3mm pearls, and form the beads into a ring by sewing through all four pearls again, leaving an 8-in. tail. Sew through the first pearl again [**fig. 1**].

2 Round 2: Pick up an 8º seed bead, and sew through the next pearl. Repeat three times, and step up through the first 8º picked up in this step [**fig. 2**].

3 Round 3: Pick up an 8º, and sew through the next 8º in the previous round. Repeat three times, and step up through the first 8º picked up in this step [**fig. 3**]. Sew through all four 8ºs in round 3 once, and through the first 8º again. Snug up the beads so round 3 sits on top of round 1 [**fig. 4**].

4 Round 4: Pick up an 11º seed bead, and sew through the next 8º in the previous round. Repeat three times, step up through the first 11º picked up in this step, and sew through the adjacent 8º picked up in round 2 [**fig. 5**].

5 Round 5: Pick up an 11º, an 8º, and an 11º, and sew through the next 8º in round 2. Repeat three times. Reinforce the thread path to secure. End the working and tail threads [**fig. 6**].

Tools & Materials
For all accessories

Tools/supplies
- Fireline 6 lb. test
- Beading needles, #12
- Thread burner
- Scissors
- 2 pairs of chainnose or bentnose pliers (or one of each)

Single-Sided Pearl Component
- **4** 3mm pearls (Swarovski 5810, powder blue)
- **12** 8º seed beads (Miyuki 2071, deep blue wine berry matte)
- **16** 11º seed beads (Miyuki 2444, blue gray rainbow gold luster)

Double-Sided Pearl Component
- **8** 3mm pearls (Swarovski 5810, powder blue)
- **8** 8º seed beads (Miyuki 2071, deep blue wine berry matte)
- **16** 11º seed beads (Miyuki 2444, blue gray rainbow gold luster)

Materials for Necklace, Bracelet, and Earrings on page 27

Legend:
- 3mm crystal pearl
- 8º seed bead
- 11º seed bead, color A
- 11º seed bead, color B
- ⅛-in. 20-gauge bright aluminum jump ring
- 3/32-in. 20-gauge bright aluminum jump ring

►TIP While Japanese seed beads are known for their uniformity, as you bead, be on the lookout for any bead that is misshapen or has a narrow hole and discard it. A misshapen bead can skew a design. The beadwork just won't sit right as subsequent beads are woven into the pattern. When a bead has a narrow hole, multiple thread passes through the bead may become a problem and one too many passes will break the bead.

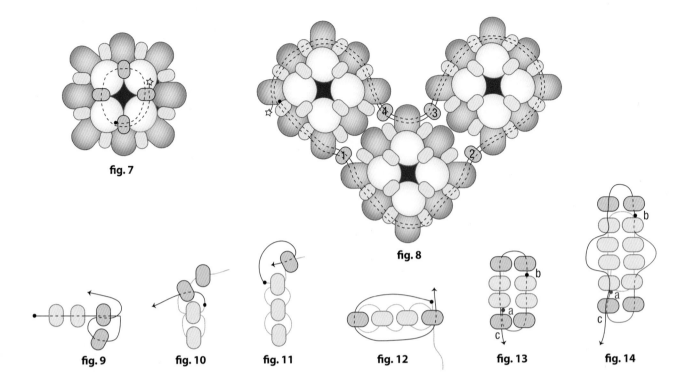

fig. 7

fig. 8

fig. 9

fig. 10

fig. 11

fig. 12

fig. 13

fig. 14

Double-Sided

1 Make a Single-Sided Pearl Component, following steps 1–5 of "Pearl Component, Single-Sided" with the following modifications: In step 3, replace the 8º seed beads with 3mm pearls. In step 5, do not end the tail thread.

2 Thread a needle on the tail. Pick up an 11º, and sew through the next pearl in round 1. Repeat three times, and step up. End the thread [**fig. 7**].

Accessories

NECKLACE

Setup

1 Make nine Single-Sided Pearl Components following steps 1–5 of "Pearl Component, Single-Sided."

2 Make four Double-Sided Pearl Components following steps 1 and 2 of "Pearl Component, Double-Sided."

Pendant

1 Add 18 in. of thread to a Single-Sided Pearl Component, and exit an 8º picked up in Round 2. Join the three Single-Sided

Pearl Components by picking up a color-A 11º seed bead at the points shown along the thread path. Retrace the thread path to secure, and end both threads [**fig. 8**].

2 Make two more pendants.

Two-Column Tubular Herringbone Strap Component

1 Follow steps 2–7 in this section to make four 16-row Two-Column Tubular Herringbone Strap Components and two 32-row Two-Column Tubular Herringbone Strap Components.

Note: In step 2, I describe using ladder stitch to start a Herringbone Strap Component. You can use the method you prefer.

2 Thread a needle onto 36 in. of thread, and pick up four color-A 11º seed beads, leaving a 12-in. tail. Fold the last two beads so the holes are parallel, and sew through the second-to-last bead again [**fig. 9**]. Fold the third bead so it sits parallel to the previous bead, and sew through the third bead [**fig. 10**]. Fold the last bead so it sits parallel to the previous

bead, and sew through the last bead in the same direction [**fig. 11**]. Form the beads into a ring by sewing through the first and last bead in the ladder again [**fig. 12**].

3 Pick up two As. Sew down through next A in the previous row and up through the following A [**fig. 13, a–b**]. Pick up two As, and sew down through the next A and up through the following A. Step up through the first A picked up in this step to be in the position to start the next row [**fig. 13, b–c**].

4 Each row consists of two stitches. To work the beadwork into a tube, continue picking up two As per stitch for the number of rows needed to complete the Herringbone Strap Component, either 16 or 32 rows [**fig. 14**], stepping up at the end of each row.

5 With the working thread exiting bead 1, pick up an 8º, sew down through bead 2, and continue up through bead 3 [**fig. 15**]. To complete the connection, sew through the 8º in the opposite direction, and sew down through bead 4. Sew up through bead 1 to exit [**fig. 16**]. End the thread.

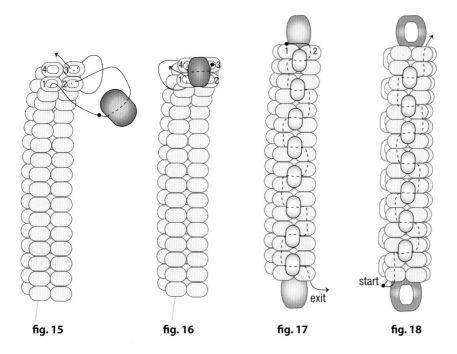

fig. 15   fig. 16   fig. 17   fig. 18

start

exit

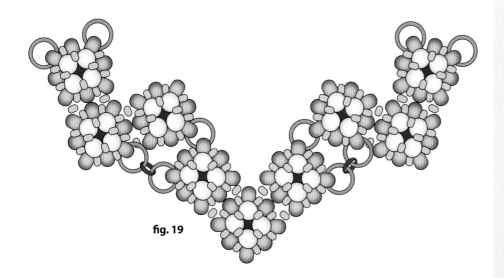

fig. 19

6 Thread a needle on the tail, and repeat step 5 to attach an 8º seed bead to the opposite strap end. End the tail.

7 To embellish the Two-Column Tubular Herringbone Strap Component, add 24 in. of thread, and sew down through bead 2. Pick up a color-B 11º seed bead, and sew down through the next two As directly under bead 1. Pick up a B, and sew down through the A adjacent to the A just exited and the next A in the column. Pick up a single B in each stitch, and zigzag as shown for the length of the column [**fig. 17**]. To embellish the next

column, rotate the strap a quarter turn to the left. With the thread positioned as shown, sew up through two As, and pick up Bs as shown [**fig. 18**]. These Bs will lie in the row between the Bs in the neighboring column. Embellish the remaining two columns.

Assembly
Attach ⅛-in. jump rings to join the three pendant components, and use two ³⁄₃₂-in. jump rings to connect the ⅛-in. jump rings as shown [**fig. 19**].

Materials
For each accessory

Necklace, 16 in.
- **9** Single-Sided Pearl Components
- **4** Double-Sided Pearl Components
- 3 grams 11º seed beads (Miyuki 2444, blue gray rainbow gold luster), color A
- Gram 11º seed beads (Matsuno 650, silver-lined ice blue AB), color B
- **60** ⅛-in. 20-gauge bright aluminum jump rings
- **2** ³⁄₃₂-in. 20-gauge bright aluminum jump rings
- 10x22mm sterling silver toggle clasp

Bracelet, 7 in.
- **23** Single-Sided Pearl Components
- **88** ⅛-in. 20-gauge bright aluminum jump rings
- **142** ³⁄₃₂-in. 20-gauge bright aluminum jump rings
- 20x6mm rhodium-plated 3-loop spring clasp

Earrings, 1¼ in.
- **6** single-sided pearl components
- **16** ⅛-in. 20-gauge bright aluminum jump rings
- **36** ³⁄₃₂-in. 20-gauge bright aluminum jump rings
- Pair of silver-plated earring findings with rhinestones

▶**TIP** To make a longer necklace, increase the number of rows in the 32-row Strap Components, or use an extender chain and a lobster claw clasp instead of a toggle clasp.

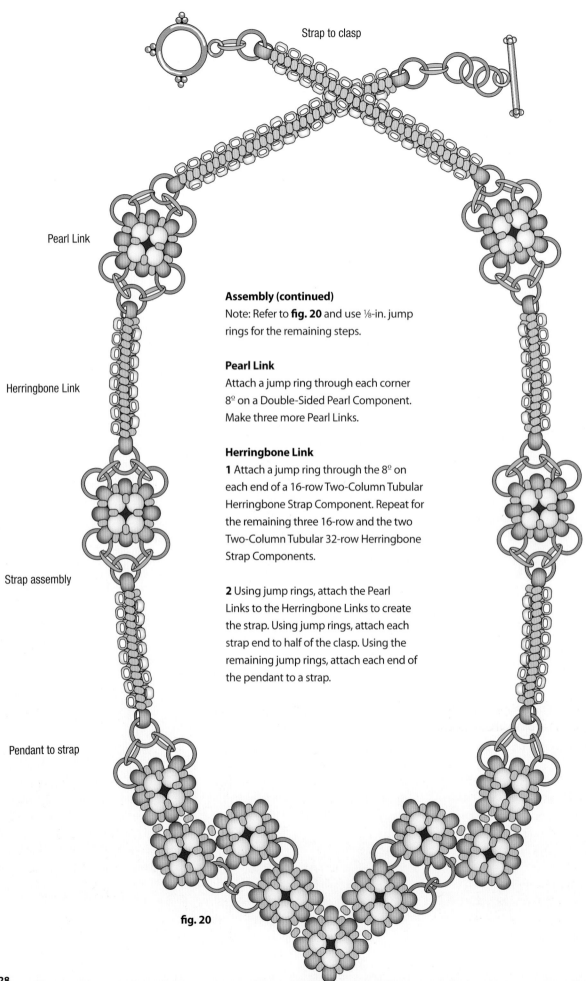

Strap to clasp

Pearl Link

Herringbone Link

Strap assembly

Pendant to strap

Assembly (continued)
Note: Refer to **fig. 20** and use ⅛-in. jump rings for the remaining steps.

Pearl Link
Attach a jump ring through each corner 8º on a Double-Sided Pearl Component. Make three more Pearl Links.

Herringbone Link
1 Attach a jump ring through the 8º on each end of a 16-row Two-Column Tubular Herringbone Strap Component. Repeat for the remaining three 16-row and the two Two-Column Tubular 32-row Herringbone Strap Components.

2 Using jump rings, attach the Pearl Links to the Herringbone Links to create the strap. Using jump rings, attach each strap end to half of the clasp. Using the remaining jump rings, attach each end of the pendant to a strap.

fig. 20

BRACELET

Setup

Make 23 Single-Sided Pearl Components following steps 1–5 of "Pearl Component, Single-Sided."

Bracelet Link

Using eight ⅛-in. jump rings, attach three Single-Sided Pearl Components [**fig. 21**]. Attach 12 ³⁄₃₂-in. jump rings to the ⅛-in. jump rings as shown [**fig. 22**]. Attach six ³⁄₃₂-in. jump rings to the 12 ³⁄₃₂-in. jump rings to complete the Bracelet Link [**fig. 23**].

End Link

Using seven ⅛-in. jump rings, attach two Single-Sided Pearl Components [**fig. 24**]. Attach eight ³⁄₃₂-in. jump rings to the ⅛-in. jump rings as shown [**fig. 25**]. Attach four ³⁄₃₂-in. jump rings to the eight ³⁄₃₂-in. jump rings to complete the End Link [**fig. 26**].

Assembly [fig. 27]

Attach the End Link to half of the clasp using two ³⁄₃₂-in. and two ⅛-in. jump rings. Using ⅛-in. jump rings, attach the other end of the End Link to a Bracelet Link. Continue to build the bracelet, attaching all the Bracelet Links in the same manner. Attach the last Bracelet Link to the other clasp half using two ³⁄₃₂-in. and two ⅛-in. jump rings.

EARRINGS

Setup

Make six Single-Sided Pearl Components following steps 1–5 of "Pearl Component, Single-Sided."

Earring Component

An Earring Component is a Bracelet Link rotated 90 degrees. Make two Earring Components, following "Bracelet, Bracelet Link."

Assembly [fig. 28]

Position the Earring Components as shown. Attach an earring finding to each earring.

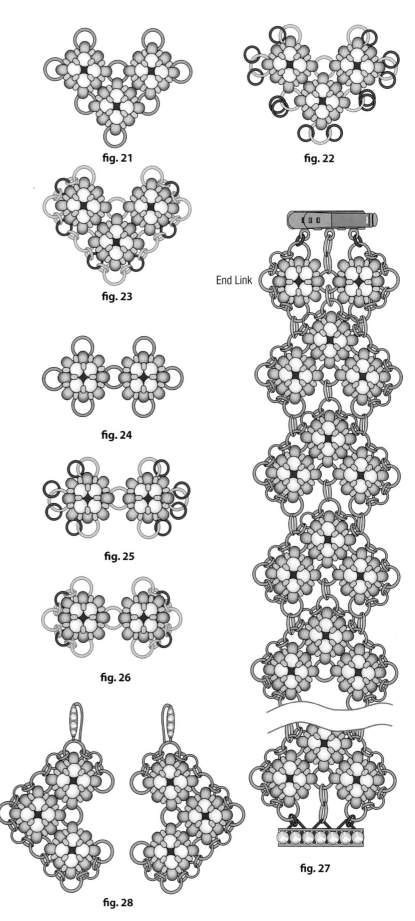

fig. 21

fig. 22

fig. 23

fig. 24

fig. 25

fig. 26

End Link

fig. 27

fig. 28

Out of Idleness

This piece was created at the start of a new chapter in my life, so it is fitting to be among the first pieces in the first chapter of the book. A few years back, I felt a need to step back from my busy life, slow down, and live in the now rather than for the future. Made up of a repetition of a stitched component, jump rings, and chain, this piece reflects that simple way of living. It is a beautiful meditation born out of idleness.

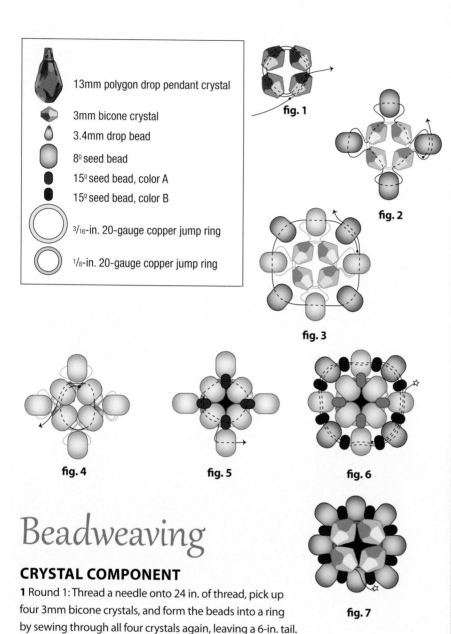

Legend:
- 13mm polygon drop pendant crystal
- 3mm bicone crystal
- 3.4mm drop bead
- 8º seed bead
- 15º seed bead, color A
- 15º seed bead, color B
- 3/16-in. 20-gauge copper jump ring
- 1/8-in. 20-gauge copper jump ring

fig. 1

fig. 2

fig. 3

fig. 4

fig. 5

fig. 6

fig. 7

Tools & Materials

For all accessories

Tools/supplies

- Fireline 6 lb. test
- Beading needles, #12
- Thread burner
- Scissors
- **2** pairs of chainnose or bentnose pliers (or one of each)
- Flush cutters
- Ruler (optional, to measure chain if using an alternate chain style)

Crystal Component

- **4** 3mm bicone crystals (Swarovski 5328, copper)
- **12** 8º seed beads (Miyuki 2035, matte metallic khaki iris)
- **4** 15º seed beads (Toho 502, raspberry bronze metallic), color A
- **8** 15º seed beads (Miyuki 229, teal-lined olive), color B

Materials for Necklace, Bracelet, and Earrings on page 32

Beadweaving

CRYSTAL COMPONENT

1 Round 1: Thread a needle onto 24 in. of thread, pick up four 3mm bicone crystals, and form the beads into a ring by sewing through all four crystals again, leaving a 6-in. tail. Sew through the first 3mm again [**fig. 1**].

2 Round 2: Pick up an 8º seed bead, and sew through the next 3mm crystal. Repeat three times, and step up through the first 8º picked up in this step [**fig. 2**].

3 Round 3: Pick up an 8º, and sew through the next 8º in the previous round. Repeat three times, and step up through the first 8º picked up in this step [**fig. 3**]. Sew through all four 8ºs in round 3 once, and sew through the first 8º again. Snug up the beads so round 3 sits on top of round 1 [**fig. 4**].

4 Round 4: Pick up a color-A 15º seed bead, and sew through the next 8º in the previous round. Repeat three times, and step down to round 2, exiting the nearest 8º [**fig. 5**].

5 Round 5: Pick up a color-B 15º seed bead, an 8º, and a B, and sew through the next 8º in round 2. Repeat three times [**fig. 6**]. Retrace the thread path, snug up the beads, and end the threads [**fig. 7**].

Materials

For each accessory

Necklace, 18 in.
- **22** Crystal Components
- 13mm crystal polygon drop pendant (Swarovski 6015, copper)
- **115** ⅛-in. 20-gauge copper jump rings
- ³⁄₁₆-in. 20-gauge copper jump ring
- 19 in. 3.5x3mm oval-and-figure-8 copper-plated chain
- 15x12mm antique-copper-plated pewter beaded 2-loop clasp

Bracelet, 7¾ in.
- **8** Crystal Components
- **36** ⅛-in. 20-gauge copper jump rings
- 8 in. 3.5x3mm oval-and-figure-8 copper-plated chain
- 15x12mm antique-copper-plated pewter beaded 2-loop clasp

Earrings, 1¼ in.
- **2** Crystal Components
- **22** ⅛-in. 20-gauge copper jump rings
- 4 in. 3.5x3mm oval-and-figure-8 copper-plated chain
- **2** 3.4mm drop beads (Miyuki DP2035, khaki iris matte metallic)
- Pair of copper earring findings

Accessories

NECKLACE

Setup
1 Make 22 Crystal Components following steps 1–5 of "Crystal Component."

2 Cut 16 three-link (½ in.), two nine-link (1⅞ in.), and two nine+one-link (2 in.) pieces of chain [**fig. 8**].

Assembly
1 To make the pendant, attach ⅛-in. jump rings to the four Crystal Components as shown. Using a ³⁄₁₆-in. jump ring, attach the crystal polygon drop pendant [**fig. 9**]. Using six ⅛-in. jump rings, connect the four Crystal Components [**fig. 10**].

2 All jump rings used in this step are ⅛ in. Build eight Strap Links using

jump rings and three-link chain pieces [**fig. 11**]. To attach the clasp, attach jump rings to the two lower corner 8º s in a Crystal Component. Pick up a nine+one-link chain, and use a jump ring to attach it to the upper left 8º on the Crystal Component. Pick up the nine-link chain, and use a jump ring to attach it to the upper right 8º.

Note: The slightly longer length of chain is positioned on the outside of the strap to allow the necklace to drape correctly around the neck.

3 Attach the other end of each chain to the ring portion of the clasp. Repeat to connect the bar portion of the clasp, reversing the positioning of the longer chain segment to the upper right and the shorter to the upper left. Use jump rings to attach the Strap Links and to attach the pendant to the strap [**fig. 12**].

 Three-link

 Nine-link

Nine+one-link

The lengths of the chain pieces are counted by the number of oval links.

fig. 8

fig. 9

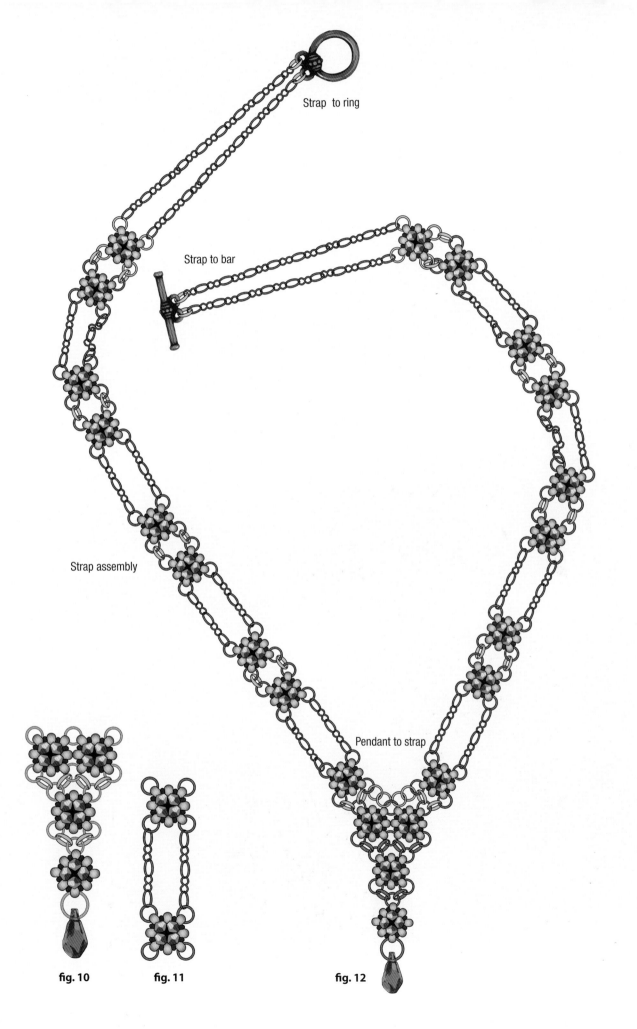

Strap to ring

Strap to bar

Strap assembly

Pendant to strap

fig. 10   **fig. 11**   **fig. 12**

fig. 14

BRACELET

Setup

1 Make eight Crystal Components following steps 1–5 of "Crystal Component."

2 Cut 18 two-link (⅜ in.) pieces of chain [**fig. 13**].

Assembly

Build the bracelet band using jump rings and two-link pieces of chain. Using jump rings, attach the chain ends to the clasp [**fig. 14**].

EARRINGS

Setup

1 Make two Crystal Components following steps 1–5 of "Crystal Component."

2 Cut four two-link (⅜ in.) and two five-link (1 in.) pieces of chain [**fig. 15**]. (If you are using an alternate chain style, be sure to use an odd number of links that measure as close as possible to 1 in. in place of the five-link chain piece.)

Two-link

fig. 13

Five-link

fig. 15

Assembly

1 Thread a jump ring through the lower left corner 8º of a Crystal Component. Attach a two-link and then a five-link chain, placing the shorter chain on the left, and close the jump ring [**fig. 16**].

2 Thread a jump ring through the upper left corner 8º. Attach the end link of the shorter chain, and close the jump ring [**fig. 17**].

3 Thread a jump ring through the lower right corner 8º. Attach the other end of the long chain and a two-link chain, and close the jump ring. Thread a jump ring through the upper right 8º. Attach the end link of the two-link chain [**fig. 18**].

4 Attach four jump rings, one to each inner portion of the jump rings at each corner 8º [**fig. 19**].

5 Join the two upper jump rings with a third. Thread a jump ring through the third oval link in the five-link chain and through the two lower jump rings [**fig. 20**]. (If you are using an alternate chain style, thread the jump ring through the middle link in the chain.)

6 Thread a 3.4mm drop bead on a new jump ring. Attach the jump ring to the third oval link in the five-link chain. (If you are using an alternate style chain, attach the jump ring to the middle link in the chain.) Attach an earring finding to the upper center jump ring [**fig. 21**]. Assemble a second earring.

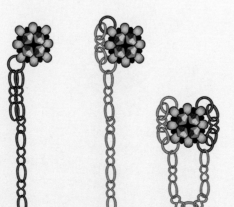

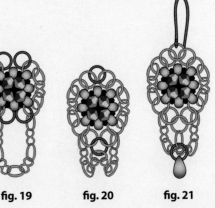

fig. 16   fig. 17   fig. 18   fig. 19   fig. 20   fig. 21

Wild Tile

The lively colors, the simple expressive shapes of the beaded tiles, and the flowing lines of the chain tassels in this set remind me of the bright colors, raw shapes, and expressive lines used by painters Henri Matisse and André Derain. This style of painting was called Fauvist, from *les fauves*, meaning the wild beasts. This is my homage to the Fauvist style.

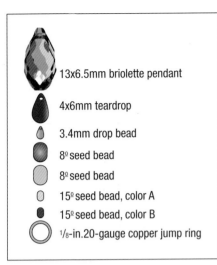

13x6.5mm briolette pendant

4x6mm teardrop

3.4mm drop bead

8º seed bead

8º seed bead

15º seed bead, color A

15º seed bead, color B

1/8-in. 20-gauge copper jump ring

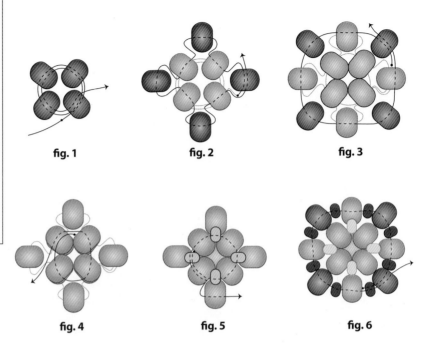

fig. 1   **fig. 2**   **fig. 3**

fig. 4   **fig. 5**   **fig. 6**

Beadweaving

TILE

1 Round 1: Thread a needle onto 30 in. of thread, pick up four 8º seed beads, and form the beads into a ring by sewing through all four 8º's again, leaving a 10-in. tail. Sew through the first 8º again. Do not knot the tail thread **[fig. 1]**.

2 Round 2: Pick up an 8º, and sew through the next 8º in the previous round. Repeat three times, and step up through the first 8º picked up in this step **[fig. 2]**.

3 Round 3: Pick up an 8º, and sew through the next 8º in the previous round. Repeat three times, and step up through the first 8º picked up in this step **[fig. 3]**. Sew through all four beads in round 3 once and the next one again. Snug up the beads so round 3 sits on top of round 1 **[fig. 4]**.

4 Round 4: Pick up a color-A 15º seed bead, and sew through the next 8º in round 3. Repeat three times, step up through the first A exited in this step, and sew down to the nearest adjacent 8º in round 2 **[fig. 5]**.

5 Round 5: Pick up a color-B 15º, an 8º, and a B, and sew through the next 8º in round 2. Repeat three times, and step up through the first B and 8º picked up in this step **[fig. 6]**.

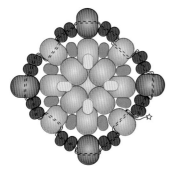

fig. 7

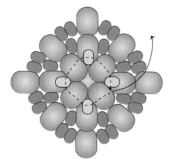

fig. 8

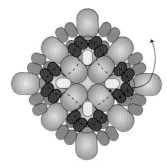

fig. 9

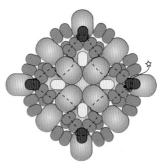

fig. 10

6 Round 6: Pick up two Bs, an 8º, and two Bs, and sew through the next 8º in round 5. Repeat three times, and retrace the thread path through the beads in round 6 again to reinforce. End the working thread [**fig. 7**].

7 Thread a needle on the tail, pick up an A, and sew through the next 8º in round 1. Repeat three times, but do not step up at the end of the round [**fig. 8**].

8 Pick up four Bs. Sew through the next 8º in round 1. Repeat three times. Step up through the first B picked up in this step [**fig. 9**].

9 Pick up a B. Sew down through the next two Bs, the next 8º in round 1, and sew up through the next two Bs. Repeat three times, and step up through the first B picked up in this step. End the tail [**fig. 10**].

▶**TIP** The stitched Tiles in this set are reversible. You can choose which side to show when you wear the necklace or bracelet. The choice is yours as well when you assemble the earrings—and they don't have to match!

Tools & Materials
For all accessories

Tools/supplies

- Fireline 6 lb. test
- Beading needles, #12
- Thread burner
- Scissors
- **2** pairs of chainnose or bentnose pliers (or one of each)
- Flush cutters
- Ruler (optional, to measure chain if using an alternate chain style)

Tile

- **20** 8º seed beads (Miyuki 645, dyed dark rose silver-lined alabaster)
- **8** 15º seed beads (Toho PF557F, permanent finish galvanized gold matte), color A
- **44** 15º seed beads (Toho 502, raspberry bronze metallic), color B

Materials for Necklace, Bracelet, and Earrings on page 39

fig. 11

fig. 12

fig. 13

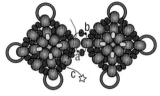

fig. 14

Wirework

TWO-RING LINK

Attach a jump ring to two opposite corner 8ºs on a Tile [**fig. 11**].

THREE-RING LINK

Attach a jump ring to three corner 8ºs on a Tile [**fig. 12**].

FOUR-RING LINK

Attach a jump ring to each of the four corner 8ºs on a Tile [**fig. 13**].

Accessories

NECKLACE

Setup

1 Make 23 Tiles following steps 1–9 of "Tile."

2 Make 11 Two-Ring Links following "Two-Ring Link."

3 Make 10 Four-Ring Links following "Four-Ring Link."

4 Make two Three-Ring Links following "Three-Ring Link."

5 Cut one 11-link (3½ in.), one 23-link (2½ in.), and one 31-link (1¼ in.) piece of chain.

Assembly

1 To join Three-Ring Links, thread a needle onto 8 in. of thread, and make a half-hitch knot to secure the working thread in one of the two Three-Ring Links, exiting the corner 8º without a jump ring [**fig. 14, a**]. Pick up a 15º, and sew through the corresponding 8º in the adjoining Three-Ring Link [**fig. 14, a–b**]. Pick up a 15º, and sew through the 8º your thread exited on the first Three-Ring Link [**fig. 14, b–c**]. End the threads.

2 Using jump rings, attach the 8ºs, the 3.4mm drop beads, and the 4x6mm teardrop beads to the three chains as shown. Attach the briolette pendant to the end link of the 3½-in. chain [**fig. 15**].

3 Open a jump ring on a Two-Ring Link. Attach the three chains to make the Tassel Link, and close the jump ring. Use jump rings to join the remaining necklace components. Attach the Tassel Link to the joined Three-Ring Links [**fig. 16**].

4 Assemble the strap by alternating the reversed sides of the Two-Ring and Four-Ring Links. Attach the strap ends to the clasp [**fig. 16**].

5 Create four dangles by attaching a 4x6mm teardrop to each of four jump rings, and attach each dangle as shown [**fig. 16**].

fig. 15

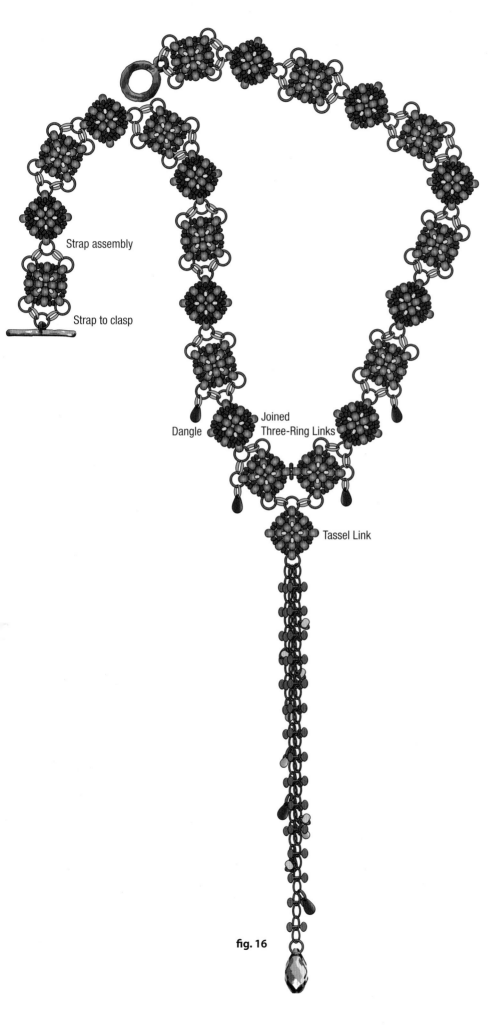

Strap assembly

Strap to clasp

Joined
Three-Ring Links

Dangle

Tassel Link

fig. 16

Materials

For each accessory

Necklace, 18 in.

- **23** Tiles

- 13x6.5mm briolette pendant (Swarovski 6010, crystal copper)

- **7** 4x6mm teardrops (Czech glass, fuchsia AB)

- **3** 3.4mm drop beads (Miyuki 03, pink-lined smoky amethyst)

- **5** 8º seed beads (Toho PF557F, permanent finish galvanized gold matte)

- **2** 15º seed beads (Toho 502, raspberry bronze metallic)

- **130** ⅛-in. 20-gauge copper jump rings

- 9 in. 3mm oval copper-plated chain to make 1 tassel

- 10x18mm hammered copper toggle clasp

Bracelet, 7¾ in.

- **9** Tiles

- **47** ⅛-in. 20-gauge copper jump rings

- 10x18mm hammered copper toggle clasp

Earrings, 1¼ in.

- **2** Tiles

- **4** 4x6mm teardrops (Czech glass, fuchsia AB)

- **2** 3.4mm drop beads (Miyuki 03, pink-lined smoky amethyst)

- **6** 8º seed beads (Toho PF471, permanent galvanized gold matte)

- **16** ⅛-in. 20-gauge copper jump rings

- 5 in. 3mm oval copper-plated chain to make 2 tassels

- Pair of copper earring findings

Band to clasp

Band assembly

fig. 17

▶TIP A 3.4mm drop bead is threaded onto a jump ring as part of the necklace and earring assembly. These small drops vary quite a bit in shape, and the holes are not uniformly sized. You may need to try several drops before you find one with an opening large enough for the jump ring to fit through.

BRACELET
Setup
1 Make nine Tiles following steps 1–9 of "Tile."

2 Make five Two-Ring Links following "Two-Ring Link."

3 Make four Four-Ring Links following "Four-Ring Link."

Assembly [fig. 17]
Use jump rings to make the bracelet band, alternate attaching the reverse sides of the Two-Ring Links and Four-Ring Links. Use the remaining jump rings to attach one half of the clasp to each of the band ends.

EARRINGS
Setup
1 Make two Tiles following steps 1–9 of "Tile."

2 Cut two three-link (¼ in.), two five-link (½ in.), and two nine-link (1 in.) pieces of chain.

Assembly
1 Using jump rings, attach the 8°s, the 3.4mm drop beads, and the 4x6mm teardrop beads to the three chains as shown [**fig. 18**].

2 Attach a jump ring to two opposite corner 8°s in a Tile. Before closing one of the jump rings, attach the chains to form a tassel. Attach an earring finding [**fig. 19**]. Assemble a second earring, reversing the order of the chains when forming the tassel.

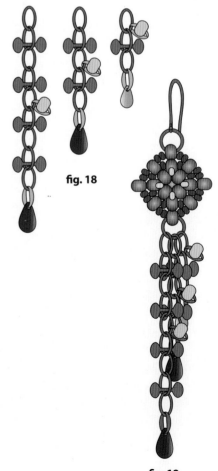

fig. 18

fig. 19

40

Count Your Blossoms

I have many amazing people in my life, and I count each as a magnificent blessing. What are you thankful for? Think about using this jewelry set as a physical reminder to be grateful for your blessings. Assign a blessing to each blossom as you stitch it.

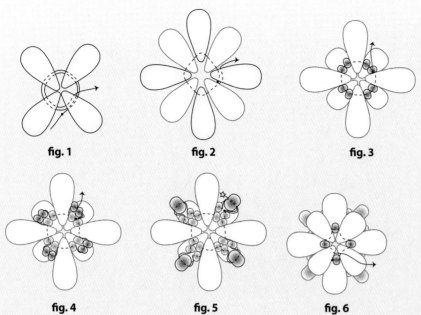

fig. 1   fig. 2   fig. 3

fig. 4   fig. 5   fig. 6

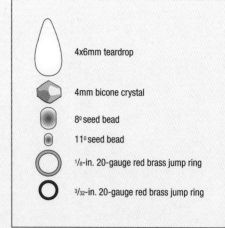

4x6mm teardrop

4mm bicone crystal

8° seed bead

11° seed bead

1/8-in. 20-gauge red brass jump ring

3/32-in. 20-gauge red brass jump ring

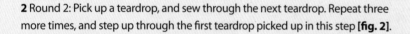

fig. 7

Beadweaving

BLOSSOM

1 Round 1: Thread a needle onto 30 in. of thread, pick up four teardrop beads, and form the beads into a ring by sewing through all four teardrops again, leaving a 12-in. tail. Step up through the first teardrop bead **[fig. 1]**.

2 Round 2: Pick up a teardrop, and sew through the next teardrop. Repeat three more times, and step up through the first teardrop picked up in this step **[fig. 2]**.

3 Round 3: Pick up two 11° seed beads, and sew through the next teardrop. Repeat three more times, and step up through the first 11° picked up in this step **[fig. 3]**.

4 Round 4: Pick up two 11°s, and sew through the next teardrop bead in round 2 and the first 11° in the next set of two in round 3. Repeat three more times, and step up through the next 11° in round 3 and the first 11° picked up in this step **[fig. 4]**.

5 Round 5: Pick up an 8° seed bead, and sew through the next 11° in round 4, the following teardrop, the 11° in round 3, and the next 11° in round 4. Repeat three more times, and step up through the first 8° picked up in this step. End the working thread **[fig. 5]**.

6 Thread a needle on the tail, pick up an 11°, and sew through the next teardrop in round 1. Repeat three more times **[fig. 6]**.

7 Pick up a 4mm bicone crystal, and sew through the teardrop directly opposite the teardrop the thread is exiting. Sew through the next 11° and the following teardrop. Sew through the 4mm bicone again and the teardrop directly opposite the one the thread is exiting. Sew through the next 11° and the following teardrop. End the tail **[fig. 7]**.

Wirework

FIGURE-8 LINK

1 To make a Large Figure-8 Link, use a US No. 8 knitting needle as a mandrel. To make a Small Figure-8 Link, use a US No. 3 knitting needle. Cut the length of 20-gauge wire specified in the instructions for the accessory you are making. Leaving a 1-in. wire tail, hold your thumb against the tail, and brace the wire against the needle **[A]**. Begin to coil, rotating your hand away from your body and making two complete wraps around the mandrel. On the next wrap, angle the motion slightly forward to create a small space between the next set of coils. Wrap the wire around the mandrel until you have two more uniform coils flush against one another. Continue in this manner, angling the wire forward between every two coils **[B]**, until you reach the end of the wire.

2 Remove the coiled wire from the mandrel. Using flush cutters, detach the separated coils by cutting at the midpoint of the angled portion of each wire section **[C]**. Pick up a cut coil, and use flush cutters to trim one end **[D]**. Place the cutters as shown and trim the other end **[E]**. Once cut, the coil resembles a split ring **[F]**.

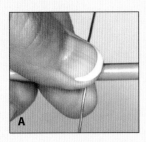
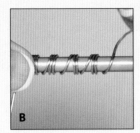
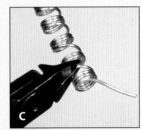

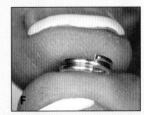
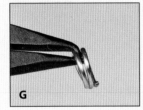
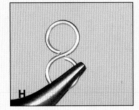

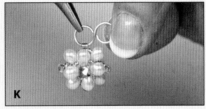

Tools & Materials
For all accessories

Tools/supplies
- Fireline 6 lb. test
- Beading needles, #12
- Thread burner
- Scissors
- Chainnose or bentnose pliers
- Split-ring pliers
- Flush cutters
- **2** knitting needles (US No. 8 and US No. 3)

Blossom
- **8** 4x6mm teardrop beads (Czech glass, cream or pearl color)
- 4mm bicone crystal (Preciosa 451 69 302, golden flare)
- **4** 8º seed beads (Toho 994, gold-lined rainbow crystal)
- **20** 11º seed beads (Toho 994, gold-lined rainbow crystal)

Materials for Necklace, Bracelet, and Earrings on page 45

3 Using split-ring pliers, open a gap in the coil by closing the tips of the jaws between the coils directly opposite the point where the two coiled ends meet **[G]**. Using your fingers or pliers, open the coil to create a Figure-8 Link **[H]**. Repeat steps 1–3 to make additional links, if necessary.

Attaching a Figure-8 Link to a Blossom
To prevent the Figure-8 Link from distorting, use your thumb and forefinger to hold one end of the link steady, and use bentnose or chainnose pliers to move the other end away from you **[I]**. Thread the open end of the Figure-8 Link through the desired 8º bead on the Blossom **[J]**. To close the link, use the pliers to move the open link back to its original position **[K]**.

Accessories

NECKLACE
Setup
1 Make 20 Blossoms following steps 1–7 of "Blossom."

2 Cut two 30-in. pieces of wire and make 21 Large Figure-8 Links, following steps 1–3 of "Figure-8 Link."

3 Cut 40 in. of wire and make 21 Small Figure-8 Links, following steps 1–3 of "Figure-8 Link."

Assembly [fig. 8]
Align the Blossoms by orienting the center crystals in the same direction. Connect the Large and Small Figure-8 Links to Blossoms, following "Attaching a Figure-8 Link to a Blossom." Using two ⅛-in. jump

> **TIP** The diameter of a US No. 8 knitting needle is 5mm; a No. 3 is 3.25mm in diameter. Use any cylinders in these sizes as mandrels to form the links.

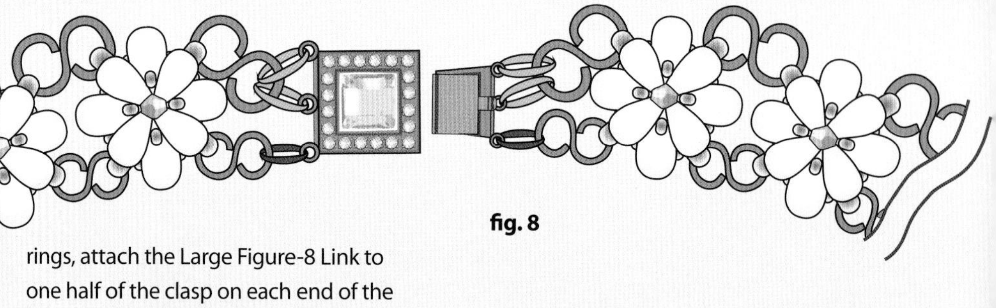

Materials

For each accessory

Necklace, 16 in.
- **20** Blossoms
- 9 ft. 20-gauge red brass wire to make 21 Large Figure-8 Links and 21 Small Figure-8 Links
- **4** ⅛-in. 20-gauge red brass jump rings
- **2** ³⁄₃₂-in. 20-gauge red brass jump rings
- 11.5x11.5mm gold-plated 3-row spring clasp

Bracelet, 7¼ in.
- **8** Blossoms
- 3 ft. 20-gauge red brass wire to make 14 Small Figure-8 Links
- **10** ⅛-in. 20-gauge red brass jump rings
- **6** ³⁄₃₂-in. 20-gauge red brass jump rings
- 11.5x11.5mm gold-plated 3-row spring clasp

Earrings, 1½ in.
- **2** Blossoms
- **2** 3.4mm drop beads (Miyuki 421D, Cream Ceylon)
- 16 in. 20-gauge red brass wire to make 8 Small Figure-8 Links
- **12** ⅛-in. 20-gauge red brass jump rings
- Pair of gold-plated earring findings with rhinestones

rings, attach the Large Figure-8 Link to one half of the clasp on each end of the necklace. Using a ³⁄₃₂-in. jump ring, join the Small Figure-8 Link to one half of the clasp on each end of the necklace.

BRACELET

Setup

1 Make eight Blossoms following steps 1–7 of "Blossom."

2 Cut 29 in. of wire and make 14 Small Figure-8 Links, following steps 1–3 of "Figure-8 Link."

Assembly [fig. 9]

Align the Blossoms by orienting the center crystals in the same direction. Connect the Blossoms, following "Attaching a Figure-8 Link to a Blossom." Attach a ⅛-in. jump ring to each of the two 8⁰s on the Blossom at either end of the bracelet band. Attach ⅛-in. jump rings to the two outside rings on one half of the clasp and to the jump rings attached to the Blossom. Attach a ³⁄₃₂-in. jump ring to the center ring of the clasp and to a freestanding ⅛-in. jump ring. Attach a ³⁄₃₂-in. jump ring to the jump rings attached to the Blossom and to the freestanding jump ring. Repeat the attachment on the other end of the bracelet with the other half of the clasp.

EARRINGS

Setup

1 Make two Blossoms following steps 1–7 of "Blossom."

2 Cut 16 in. of wire and make eight Small Figure-8 Links, following steps 1–3 of "Figure-8 Link."

Assembly [fig. 10]

Attach four Small Figure-8 Links to a Blossom, following "Attaching a Figure-8 Link to a Blossom." Attach a drop bead to a ⅛-in. jump ring. Attach five ⅛-in. jump rings and an earring finding to complete the assembly as shown. Make a second earring.

fig. 8

fig. 10

fig. 9

Broadening

This group of projects will take your wirework skills to the next level. Use jewelry pliers to form eyepins, wrapped loops, and other simple wire shapes to link the beaded components.

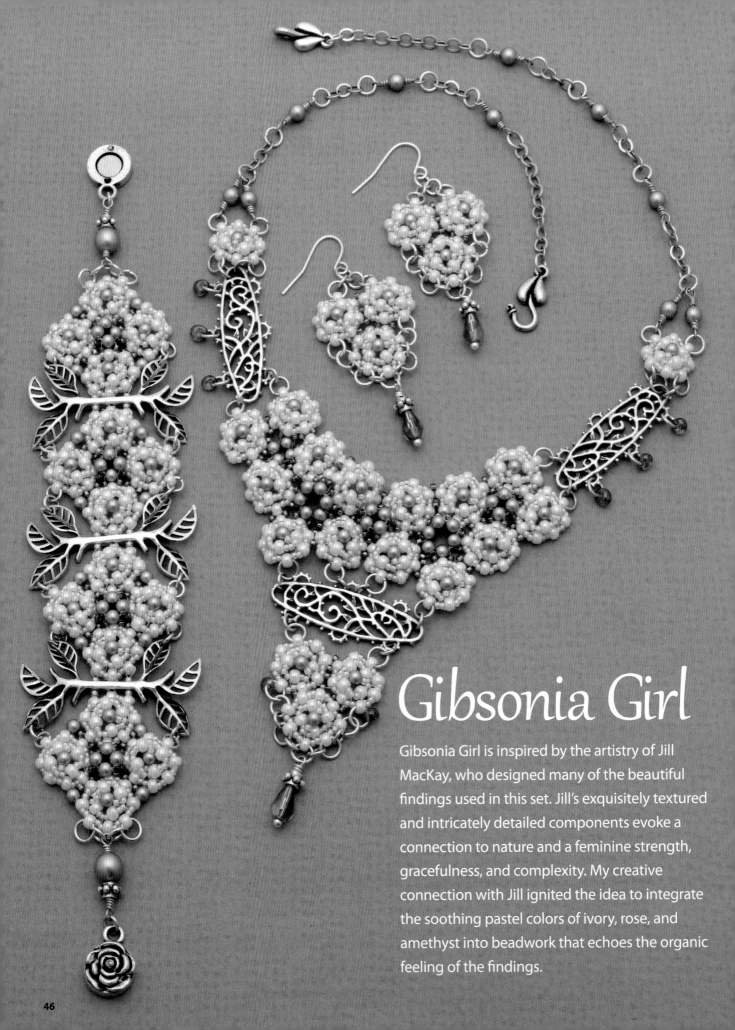

Gibsonia Girl

Gibsonia Girl is inspired by the artistry of Jill MacKay, who designed many of the beautiful findings used in this set. Jill's exquisitely textured and intricately detailed components evoke a connection to nature and a feminine strength, gracefulness, and complexity. My creative connection with Jill ignited the idea to integrate the soothing pastel colors of ivory, rose, and amethyst into beadwork that echoes the organic feeling of the findings.

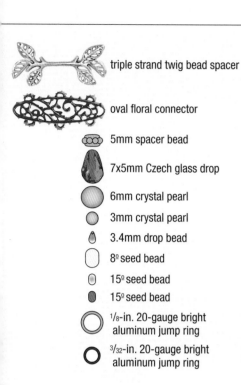

triple strand twig bead spacer

oval floral connector

5mm spacer bead

7x5mm Czech glass drop

6mm crystal pearl

3mm crystal pearl

3.4mm drop bead

8º seed bead

15º seed bead

15º seed bead

1/8-in. 20-gauge bright aluminum jump ring

3/32-in. 20-gauge bright aluminum jump ring

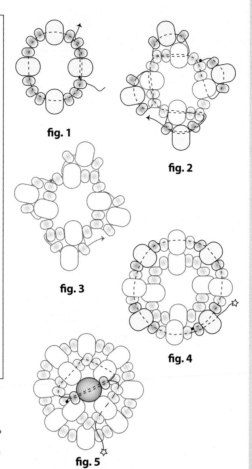

fig. 1

fig. 2

fig. 3

fig. 4

fig. 5

Beadweaving

ROSE

1 Round 1: Thread a needle onto 24 in. of thread, and pick up an 8º seed bead, three 15º seed beads, an 8º, three 15ºs, an 8º, three 15ºs, an 8º, and three 15ºs. Form the beads into a ring by sewing through all the beads again, leaving an 8-in. tail. Step up through the first 8º and the next two 15ºs picked up in this step **[fig. 1]**.

2 Round 2: Pick up a 15º, an 8º, and a 15º, and sew back through the 8º and two 15ºs your thread exited at the start of this round. Sew through the next 15º, 8º, and two 15ºs. Repeat three times. Step up through the 15º, an 8º, and the 15º just picked up **[fig. 2]**.

3 Round 3: Flip the beadwork over to work in a counterclockwise direction **[fig. 3]**. The Rose will become slightly concave as you add beads to the round. Pick up a 15º, an 8º, and a 15º, and sew through the next 15º, 8º, and 15º. Repeat three times. Exit the first 8º picked up in this step, and end the working thread **[fig. 4]**.

4 Thread a needle on the tail. Pick up a 15º, a 3mm pearl, and a 15º, and sew through the 8º opposite the 8º the thread is exiting. Sew through the beadwork as shown. End the tail **[fig. 5]**.

▶ **TIP** I keep a few worn needles handy to use as tools. When thread paths crowd the hole of a connecting 8º, I slip a used needle in to open up space for the jump ring.

Tools & Materials
For all accessories

Tools/supplies
- Fireline 6 lb. test
- Beading needles, #12
- Thread burner
- Scissors
- **2** pairs of chainnose or bentnose pliers (or one of each)
- Looping pliers
- Flush cutters
- Ruler

Rose
- **12** 8º seed beads (Toho 123, opaque cream luster)
- **30** 15º seed beads (Miyuki 215, blush-lined crystal)
- 3mm round pearl (Swarovski 3810, powder rose)

Rose Triangle
- **3** Roses
- **7** 15º seed beads (Miyuki 137R, silver-lined amethyst AB)

Rose Cross
- **4** Roses
- **4** 3mm round pearls (Swarovski 3810, powder rose)
- **16** 15º seed beads (Miyuki 137R, silver-lined amethyst AB)

Rose Square
- Rose Cross
- **4** 3mm round pearls (Swarovski 3810, powder rose)

Pendant Drop
- 2-in. 22-gauge silver-plated or sterling silver headpin with 1.5mm ball
- 5mm silver-plated or sterling silver spacer bead
- 7x5mm drop (Czech glass, fire-polished amethyst)

Materials for Necklace, Bracelet, and Earrings on page 49

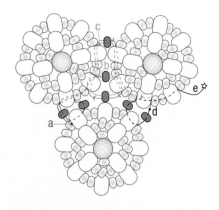

fig. 6

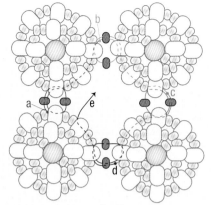

fig. 7

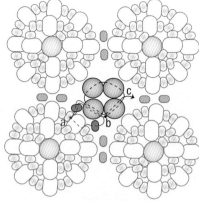

fig. 8

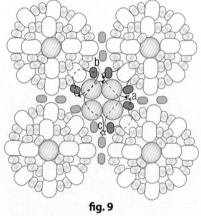

fig. 9

ROSE TRIANGLE

1 Make three Roses following steps 1–4 of "Rose."

2 Thread a needle onto 24 in. of thread. Arrange the three Roses as shown [**fig. 6**]. Secure the thread, and exit the 8º seed bead at point **a**. Pick up a 15º seed bead, and sew through the corresponding 8º in the second Rose. Pick up a 15º, and sew through the 8º your thread exited in the first Rose and the first 15º picked up. Sew through the second Rose as shown [**fig. 6, a–b**]. Pick up a 15º, and sew through the corresponding 8º in the third Rose. Pick up a 15º, and sew through the second Rose as shown [**fig. 6, b–c**]. Pick up a 15º, and sew through the second and third Roses as shown [**fig. 6, c–d**]. Pick up a 15º, and sew through the 8º in the first Rose. Pick up a 15º, sew through the third Rose as shown [**fig. 6, d–e**], and end the threads.

ROSE CROSS

1 Make four Roses following steps 1–4 of "Rose."

2 Thread a needle onto 24 in. of thread. Arrange the four Roses as shown [**fig. 7**]. Secure the thread, and exit the 8º at point **a**. Pick up a 15º, and sew through the corresponding 8º in the next Rose. Pick up a 15º, and sew through the 8º your thread exited in the first Rose and the first 15º picked up. Sew through the beadwork as shown [**fig. 7, a–b**]. Repeat to connect all four Roses [**fig. 7, b–c, c–d, d–e**].

3 Pick up a 15º, a 3mm pearl, and a 15º, and sew back through the 8º the thread is exiting, the first 15º, and the pearl just picked up [**fig. 8, a–b**]. Pick up three pearls, and form the beads into a ring by sewing through the first and second pearls picked up in this step [**fig. 8, b–c**].

4 Pick up a 15º, and sew through the 8º in the adjacent Rose. Pick up a 15º, and sew through the next two pearls as shown [**fig. 9, a–b**]. Repeat a–b for the next two Roses, and end the threads [**fig. 9, b–c**].

ROSE SQUARE

1 Make one Rose Cross following steps 1–4 of "Rose Cross."

2 Add 12 in. of thread to a "Rose Cross," exiting the 8º shown at the start point. Sew through the path as shown, picking up a 3mm pearl at each of the four points indicated. Step up through the first 3mm [**fig. 10**], and end the threads.

Wirework

PENDANT DROP

String a 7x5mm drop and 3mm silver spacer on a 2-in. headpin. Make a Pendant Drop following steps 5–7 of "Making a wrapped loop with looping pliers" (p. 21) to make a wrapped loop above the beads.

Accessories

NECKLACE

Setup

1 Make four Roses following steps 1–4 of "Rose."

2 Make one Rose Triangle following steps 1 and 2 of "Rose Triangle."

3 Make three Rose Crosses following steps 1–4 of "Rose Cross."

4 Cut six Three-Link (⅜ in.) and two 11-Link (1¼ in.) pieces of chain.

5 Make one Pendant Drop following "Pendant Drop."

6 Using 2¼ in. of wire and a 3mm pearl for each link, make 10 Pearl Links following "Making a wrapped loop with looping pliers."

Necklace Body

1 Add 36 in. of thread to a "Rose", and exit an 8º at point **a** [**fig. 11**]. Position the Rose and two Rose Crosses as shown. Pick up a 15º,

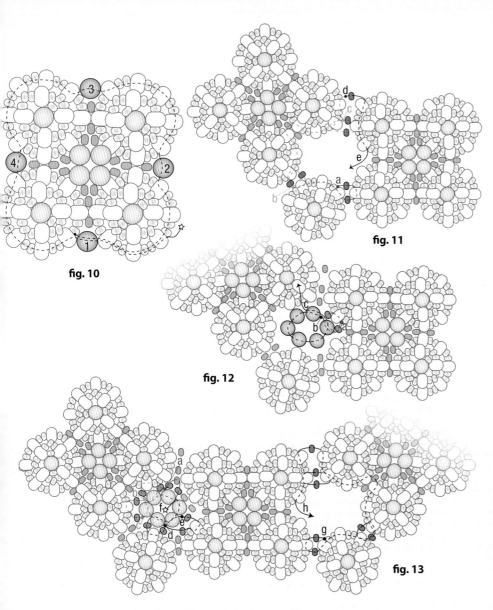

fig. 10

fig. 11

fig. 12

fig. 13

sew through the 8º in the first Rose Cross, pick up a 15º, and sew back through the 8º in the Rose. Sew through the beadwork as shown **[fig. 11, a–b]**. Pick up a 15º, and sew through the 8º in the second Rose Cross. Pick up a 15º, and sew back through the 8º in the Rose and the next 15º and 8º in the second Rose Cross. Sew through the beadwork as shown **[fig. 11, b–c]**. Pick up a 15º, sew through the 8º in the first Rose Cross, pick up a 15º, and sew back through the 8º in the second Rose Cross. Sew through the beadwork as shown **[fig. 11, c–d]**. Pick up a 15º, and sew through the beadwork as shown **[fig. 11, d–e]**.

2 Pick up a 15º, a 3mm pearl, and a 15º, and sew back through the 8º on the first Rose Cross, the 15º, and the 3mm pearl just picked up **[fig. 12, a–b]**. Pick up five 3mm pearls, and form the beads into a ring by

sewing through the first two pearls picked up in this step **[fig. 12, b–c]**.

3 Pick up a 15º, and sew through the 15º as shown. Pick up a 15º, and sew through the next two pearls **[fig. 13, a–b]**. Pick up a 15º, and sew through the 8º on the second Rose Cross. Pick up a 15º, sew back through the last pearl exited, and sew through the next pearl in the ring **[fig. 13, b–c]**. Repeat as in **b** and **c**, moving forward around the ring of pearls. End the threads **[fig. 13, c–d, d–e, e–f]**. Repeat step 1 working counterclockwise to join a third Rose Cross and a second Rose to the body **[fig. 13, g–h]**. To complete the body, repeat steps 2 and 3, working clockwise and adjusting for where the working thread is exiting at point **h**.

Materials

For each accessory

Necklace, 16½ in.
- **4** Roses
- Rose Triangle
- **3** Rose Crosses
- Pendant Drop
- **8** 3.4mm drop beads (Miyuki 303, lavender rose gold luster)
- **10** 3mm round pearls (Swarovski 3810, powder rose)
- **38** 15º seed beads (Miyuki 137R, silver-lined amethyst AB)
- 3 ft. 24-gauge titanium craft wire
- **41** ⅛-in. 20-gauge bright aluminum jump rings
- **24** ³/₃₂-in. 20-gauge bright aluminum jump rings
- 6 in. 3mm oval antique-silver-finish chain
- **3** 35x13mm sterling silver or stainless steel oval floral connectors
- Antique-silver-plated pewter leaf hook-and-eye clasp

Bracelet, 7½ in.
- **4** Rose Squares
- **2** 6mm round pearls (Swarovski 3810, powder rose)
- 7 in. 24-gauge titanium craft wire
- **4** ⅛-in. 20-gauge bright aluminum jump rings
- **30** ³/₃₂-in. 20-gauge bright aluminum jump rings
- **3** sterling silver 3-strand twig spacers
- **2** 5mm silver spacers
- 10mm silver-plated rose magnetic clasp

Earrings, 1¾ in.
- **2** Rose Triangles
- **2** Pendant Drops
- **20** ⅛-in. 20-gauge bright aluminum jump rings
- **12** ³/₃₂-in. 20-gauge bright aluminum jump rings
- Pair of sterling silver earring findings

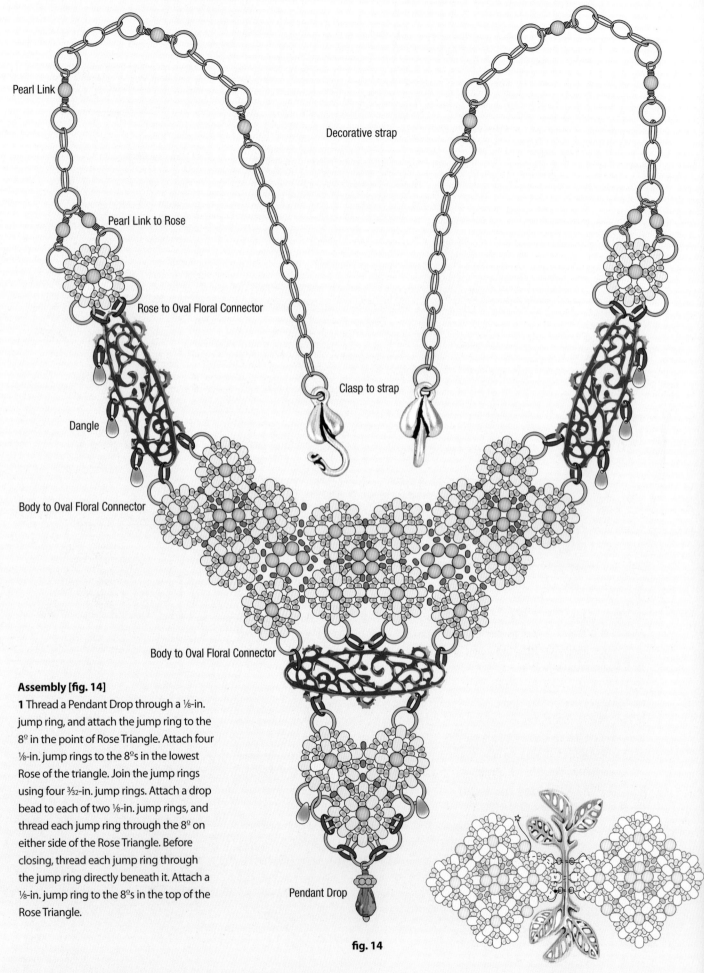

Pearl Link

Pearl Link to Rose

Decorative strap

Rose to Oval Floral Connector

Clasp to strap

Dangle

Body to Oval Floral Connector

Body to Oval Floral Connector

Assembly [fig. 14]

1 Thread a Pendant Drop through a ⅛-in. jump ring, and attach the jump ring to the 8º in the point of Rose Triangle. Attach four ⅛-in. jump rings to the 8ºs in the lowest Rose of the triangle. Join the jump rings using four ³⁄₃₂-in. jump rings. Attach a drop bead to each of two ⅛-in. jump rings, and thread each jump ring through the 8º on either side of the Rose Triangle. Before closing, thread each jump ring through the jump ring directly beneath it. Attach a ⅛-in. jump ring to the 8ºs in the top of the Rose Triangle.

Pendant Drop

fig. 14

fig. 15

2 Attach ⅛-in. jump rings to the 8⁰s in the body of the necklace. Using ³⁄₃₂-in. jump rings, join the body to the three Oval Floral Connectors and the Rose Triangle. Make six dangles by attaching a drop bead to a ³⁄₃₂-in. jump ring, and attach as shown.

3 Attach ⅛-in. jump rings to the two lower 8⁰s in each Rose. Using two ³⁄₃₂-in. jump rings, join each Rose to the Oval Floral Connectors. Attach ⅛-in. jump rings to the two upper 8⁰s in each Rose, and, before closing the jump rings, attach a Pearl Link to each jump ring. On each end, assemble the strap using ⅛-in. jump rings to join the chain pieces and Pearl Links. Attach half of the clasp to each end with a ⅛-in. jump ring.

BRACELET

Setup

1 Make four Rose Squares following steps 1–2 of "Rose Square."

2 Using a 2¾-in. piece of wire, a 3mm silver spacer, and a 6mm pearl for each link, make two Spacer Links following "Making a wrapped loop with looping pliers."

Band

Add 12 in. of thread to a Rose Square, exiting the 8⁰ shown at the start point. To join the Rose Squares, follow the thread path, sewing back and forth through each of the three holes in the Twig Spacer and picking up a 15⁰ at each point indicated **[fig. 15]**. End the threads. Repeat to join another Twig Spacer and Rose Square on the end of the bracelet band. Continue in this manner to complete the bracelet band. End the threads.

Assembly [fig. 16]

Use two ³⁄₃₂-in. jump rings to attach an end 8⁰ along the bracelet band to a hole in each outer leaf of a Twig Spacer as shown. Attach a ⅛-in. jump ring to each of the two 8⁰s on each end of the bracelet band. Using ³⁄₃₂-in. jump rings, attach a Spacer Link to each band end, and attach one half of the clasp to each Spacer Link.

EARRINGS

Setup

1 Make two Rose Triangles following steps 1 and 2 of "Rose Triangle."

2 Make two Pendant Drops following "Pendant Drop."

Assembly [fig. 17]

Thread a Pendant Drop through a ⅛-in. jump ring, and attach the jump ring to the 8⁰ in the point of a Rose Triangle. Attach a ⅛-in. jump ring to each of four 8⁰s in the lowest Rose of the triangle. Join the jump rings using four ³⁄₃₂-in. jump rings. Thread a ⅛-in. jump ring through each 8⁰ on either side of the Rose Triangle. Before closing, thread each through the jump ring directly beneath it. Attach a ⅛-in. jump ring to the 8⁰s in the top of the Rose Triangle. Attach a ³⁄₃₂-in. jump ring to each of these two jump rings and to a ⅛-in. jump ring. Attach an earring finding to the ⅛-in. jump ring. Assemble a second earring.

▶ **TIP** To make the bracelet shorter, reduce the number or size of the beads to make shorter Spacer Links, or eliminate the links altogether.

Spacer Link to clasp

Band end to Spacer Link

Twig Spacers to band

fig. 16

fig. 17

Modern Vintage

Combine a modern and exquisite use of materials with a vintage feel. This set marries two styles of gleaming stainless steel components with my dimensional stitched Crystal Pillows, which build on a variation of herringbone stitch. Pull it all together with the knowledge and experience you already have working with wrapped loops, jump rings, and chain.

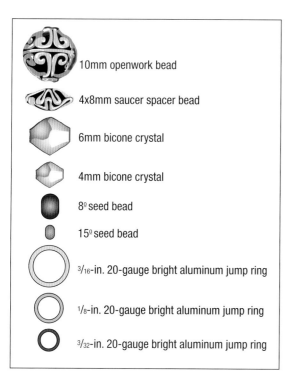

- 10mm openwork bead
- 4x8mm saucer spacer bead
- 6mm bicone crystal
- 4mm bicone crystal
- 8º seed bead
- 15º seed bead
- 3/16-in. 20-gauge bright aluminum jump ring
- 1/8-in. 20-gauge bright aluminum jump ring
- 3/32-in. 20-gauge bright aluminum jump ring

fig. 1

fig. 2

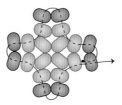

fig. 3

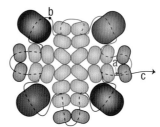

fig. 4

Tools & Materials
For all accessories

Tools/supplies
- Fireline 6 lb. test
- Beading needles, #12
- Thread burner
- Scissors
- **2** pairs of chainnose or bentnose pliers (or one of each)
- Looping pliers
- Flush cutters
- Ruler

Crystal Pillow
- **12** 4mm bicone crystals (Preciosa 451 69 302, aqua bohemica)
- **16** 8º seed beads (Miyuki 462, metallic gold iris)
- Gram 15º seed beads (Toho 999, gold-lined rainbow black diamond)

Materials for Necklace, Bracelet, and Earrings on page 55

Beadweaving

CRYSTAL PILLOW

1 Round 1: Thread a needle onto 48 in. of thread, pick up four 15º seed beads, and form the beads into a ring by sewing through all four beads again, leaving an 8-in. tail [**fig. 1**]. Sew through the first 15º again.

2 Round 2: Pick up two 15ºs, and sew through the next 15º in the previous round. Repeat three times. On the third repeat, step up through the first 15º picked up in this step [**fig. 2**].

3 Round 3: Work a herringbone stitch by picking up two 15ºs, sewing down through the next 15º in round 2, and sewing up through the following 15º. Repeat this stitch three times. On the third repeat, step up through the first 15º picked up in this step [**fig. 3**].

4 Round 4: Pick up two 15ºs, sew down through the next 15º in round 3, pick up an 8º seed bead, sew up through the next 15º, and sew down through the following 15º [**fig. 4, a–b**]. Pick up an 8º, sew up through the next 15º, pick up two 15ºs, and sew down through the following 15º. Repeat this last stitch once, pick up an 8º, and sew through the next 15º. Step up through the first 15º picked up in this step [**fig. 4, b–c**].

> ▶**TIP** The stainless steel components, from Jill MacKay, are just as beautiful but more affordable than sterling silver—and they don't tarnish.

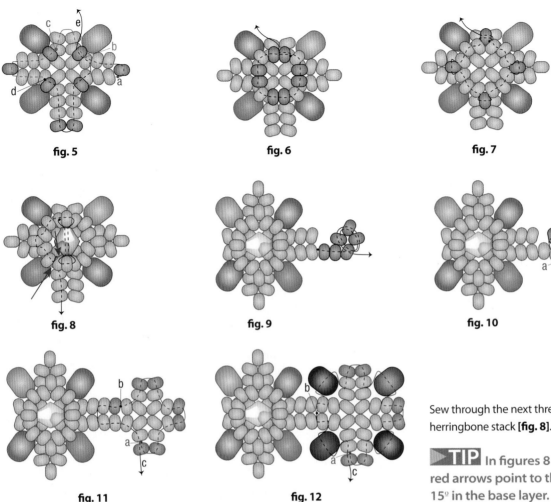

fig. 5

fig. 6

fig. 7

fig. 8

fig. 9

fig. 10

fig. 11

fig. 12

Sew through the next three 15ºs in the herringbone stack [**fig. 8**].

▶**TIP** In figures 8 and 14, red arrows point to the hidden 15º in the base layer.

5 Round 5: Pick up a 15º, and sew down through the next three 15ºs in rounds 4, 3, and 2. This bead forms a point at the end of round 4 [**fig. 5, a–b**]. Pick up a 15º. This 15º starts the raised portion of the component and sits at an angle in between each 15º in round 2. Sew up through the next two 15ºs in rounds 2 and 3, and sew down through the next two 15ºs in rounds 3 and 2 [**fig. 5, b–c**]. Pick up a 15º, and sew up through the next three 15ºs in rounds 2, 3 and 4, pick up a 15º, and sew down through the next three 15ºs in rounds 4, 3 and 2 [**fig. 5, c–d**]. Pick up a 15º, and sew up through the next three 15ºs in rounds 2, 3 and 4. Pick up two 15ºs, and sew down through the next three 15ºs in rounds 4, 3 and 2. Pick up a 15º, and sew up through the next 15º in round 2, and sew down through the following 15º in round 2. Step up through

the first raised 15º picked up in this step [**fig. 5, d–e**].

6 Pick up two 15ºs, and sew through the next raised 15º. Repeat three times. On the third repeat, step up through the first 15º picked up in this step [**fig. 6**].

7 Pick up a 15º, and sew through the next three raised 15ºs. Repeat three times. On the third repeat, step up through the first 15º picked up in this step [**fig. 7**].

8 Pick up a 4mm crystal, sew through the 15º opposite the one the thread is exiting, sew back through the 4mm and the 15º your thread exited at the start of this step. Sew through the next six raised 15ºs. Sew through the beadwork to exit the closest 15º in the base. This 15º is hard to see because it is under a raised 15º.

9 Pick up six 15ºs, skip the first two 15ºs just picked up, and sew back through the last four 15ºs to form a loop. Check that the loop is tight against the two skipped beads, and sew through the first 15º in the loop again [**fig. 9**].

10 Pick up two 15ºs, and sew through the next 15º in the loop. Repeat two times [**fig. 10, a–b**]. Pick up a 15º, sew up through the second skipped 15º in the loop created in step 9, and continue through the next two 15ºs as shown [**b–c**].

11 Pick up two 15ºs, sew down through the next 15º in the previous round, and continue up through the following 15º. Repeat two times [**fig. 11, a–b**]. Pick up a 15º, and close the gap in the base by sewing through the 15º at the end of the previous section. Sew through the beadwork as shown [**fig. 11, b–c**].

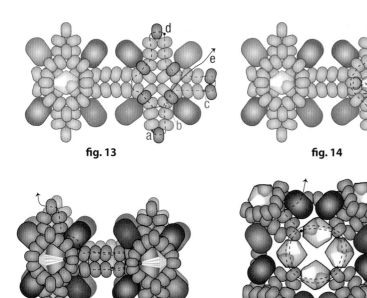

fig. 13

fig. 14

fig. 15

fig. 16

Materials

For each accessory

Necklace, 19 in.

- **4** Crystal Pillows
- **9** 10mm stainless steel openwork beads
- **18** 4x8mm stainless steel saucer spacers
- **18** 6mm bicone crystals (Preciosa 451 69 302, aqua bohemica)
- 4 ft. 24-gauge titanium craft wire
- **4** ⅛-in. 20-gauge bright aluminum jump rings
- **9** ³⁄₃₂-in. 20-gauge bright aluminum jump rings
- 27 in. 2mm sterling silver textured oval chain
- **8** 9x10mm antique-silver-plated pewter vine prong bails
- 23x19mm antique-silver-plated oval toggle clasp

Bracelet, 7¼ in.

- Crystal Pillow
- **11** 4mm bicone crystals (Preciosa 451 69 302, aqua bohemica)
- 3 ft. 24-gauge titanium craft wire
- **13** ⅛-in. 20-gauge bright aluminum jump rings
- 9 in. 2mm sterling silver textured oval chain
- 9x10mm antique-silver-plated pewter vine prong bail
- 12.5mm antique-silver-plated pewter classic toggle clasp

Earrings, 1¾ in.

- **2** Crystal Pillows
- **2** 4x8mm stainless steel saucer spacers
- **2** 6mm bicone crystals (Preciosa 451 69 302, aqua bohemica)
- **2** 4mm bicone crystals (Preciosa 451 69 302, aqua bohemica)
- 8 in. 24-gauge titanium craft wire
- **2** 9x10mm antique-silver-plated pewter vine prong bails
- Pair of sterling silver earring findings

12 Pick up two 15ºs, sew down through the next 15º in the previous round, pick up an 8º, and sew up through the following 15º. Repeat two times **[fig. 12, a–b]**. Without picking up any beads, sew up through the next 15º in the previous round. Pick up an 8º, and sew up through the next 15º in the previous round. Step up through the first 15º picked up in this step **[fig. 12, b–c]**.

13 To form a point at the end of round 4, pick up a 15º, and sew down through the next three 15ºs in rounds 4, 3, and 2 **[fig. 13, a–b]**. To start the raised portion of the section, pick up a 15º, and sew up through the next three 15ºs in rounds 2, 3, and 4 **[fig. 13, b–c]**. Pick up two 15ºs, and sew down through the next three 15ºs in rounds 4, 3, and 2. Repeat path **b–c** **[fig. 13, c–d]**. Repeat path **a–b**. Pick up a 15º, sew up through the next 15º in round 2 and sew down through the following 15º. Pick up a 15º, sew up through the next 15º in round 2, and sew down through the next 15º. Step up through the first raised 15º picked up in this step **[fig. 13, d–e]**.

14 Repeat steps 6 and 7.

15 Pick up a 4mm crystal, and sew through the 15º opposite the 15º the thread is exiting. Sew back through the crystal and the 15º your thread exited at the start of this step. Sew through the next 14 raised 15ºs. Sew through the beadwork to exit the closest 15º in the base (hidden under a raised 15º). Sew through the next three 15ºs in the herringbone stack **[fig. 14]**.

16 Repeat steps 9–15 twice to make two additional sections. End the tail thread.

17 Using the working thread, follow the thread path as shown to join the ends of the herringbone strip into a ring **[fig. 15]**.

18 Turn the ring 45 degrees. Pick up a 4mm crystal, and sew through the 15º that forms a point on the next herringbone section. Repeat for the next three sections. Retrace the thread path to reinforce, and exit through an 8º **[fig. 16]**. Flip the ring to the other side. Sew through the beadwork, and exit the nearest 15º that forms a point in the next herringbone section. Repeat the thread path to add 4mm crystals, and end the thread.

Wirework

ATTACHING A BAIL TO A CRYSTAL PILLOW

1 Pick up a 9x10mm prong bail. Using chainnose pliers, bring the prong ends closer together, leaving enough space to allow the prongs to pass over the width of the 15°s that form the space between the herringbone sections **[A]**.

2 Slide the prongs between the beads of a herringbone section on a Crystal Pillow **[B]**.

3 Rotate the bail so it sits at a 90-degree angle. Using chainnose pliers, bring the prong ends together to secure the connection to the Crystal Pillow **[C]**.

MAKING A WRAPPED LOOP AROUND A CHAIN LINK

1 Follow steps 1–3 of "Making a wrapped loop with looping pliers" (p. 21).

2 Thread the end chain link onto the open loop **[D]**.

3 Using bentnose or chainnose pliers, hold the loop to keep its shape, using another pair of bentnose or chainnose pliers tightly pull and wrap the wire around the long wire approximately 2½ times **[E]**. Trim the wrapping wire.

4 Follow Steps 5 and 6 of "Making a wrapped loop with looping pliers." If directed in the instruction step for the accessory you are making, thread the end chain link onto the open loop **[F]**.

5 Using bentnose or chainnose pliers, hold the loop to keep its shape and use another pair of pliers to tightly pull and wrap the wire filling in the space between the bead **[G]**. Flush-cut the wire end.

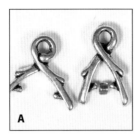
A

B

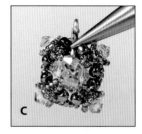
C

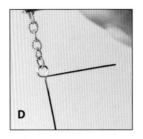
D

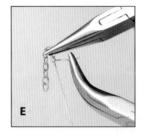
E

F

Accessories

NECKLACE
Setup

1 Make four Crystal Pillows, following steps 1–18 of "Crystal Pillow."

2 Cut one five-link (½ in.), 10 seven-link (¾ in), two 11-link (1 in.) and four 30-link (3 in.) pieces of chain.

Assembly [fig. 17]

Note: Use ³⁄₃₂-in. jump rings for all assembly except for attaching the clasp; for that, use ⅛-in. jump rings. An Openwork Link is composed of a 4-in. piece of wire, a 6mm crystal, a saucer spacer bead, and a 6mm crystal. Openwork Links are constructed between wrapped loops as chain pieces are attached. Use seven-link pieces of chain to create the upper straps, and seven-link and 11-link chain pieces to create the lower straps.

1 Make Openwork Links following steps 1–5, "Making a Wrapped Loop Around a Chain Link."

2 Make four Crystal Pillow Links by attaching two bails opposite one another on each Crystal Pillow, following steps 1–3, "Attaching a Bail to a Crystal Pillow." Place a Crystal Pillow Link between each upper and

G

lower strap, and attach it using jump rings.

3 Make the pendant using jump rings to join two Crystal Pillow Links, and attach the pendant to the lower straps.

4 Make the tassel by attaching four 30-link chain pieces to a jump ring, and attach the jump ring to an Openwork Link with a five-link piece of chain attached. Use a jump ring to attach the other end of the Openwork Link to the pendant. Use jump rings to attach each strap end to one half of the clasp.

BRACELET
Setup

1 Make one Crystal Pillow, following steps 1–18 of "Crystal Pillow."

2 Cut 22 five-link (⁵⁄₁₆ in.) pieces of chain.

3 Using a 2½-in. piece of wire and a 4mm crystal for each link, make 11 Crystal Links following "Making a wrapped loop with looping pliers" (p. 21).

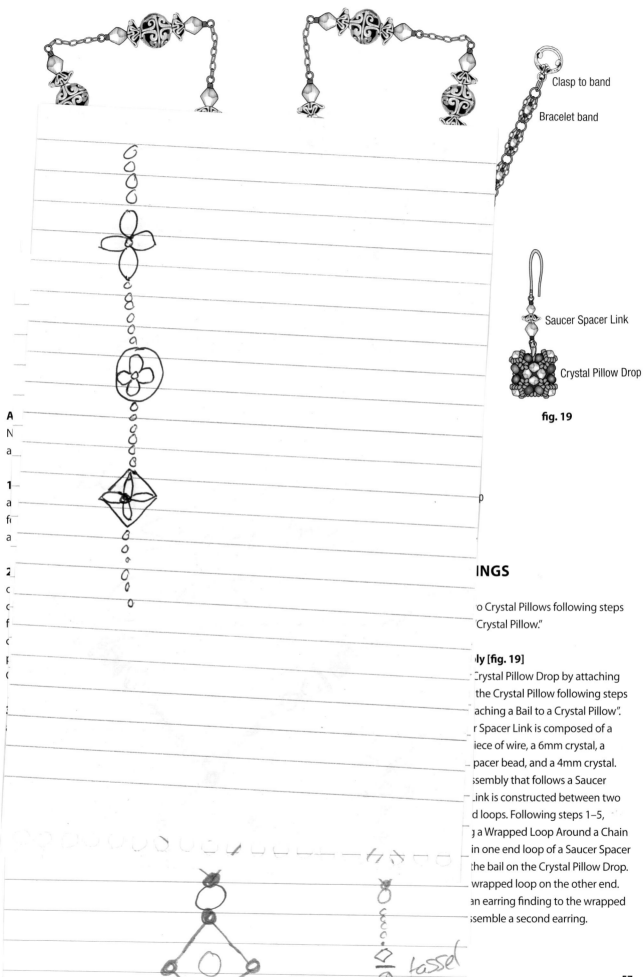

Clasp to band

Bracelet band

Saucer Spacer Link

Crystal Pillow Drop

fig. 19

A

N
a

1
a
fo
a

2
c
c
f
c

p
O

INGS

o Crystal Pillows following steps
Crystal Pillow."

ly [fig. 19]
Crystal Pillow Drop by attaching
the Crystal Pillow following steps
aching a Bail to a Crystal Pillow".
r Spacer Link is composed of a
iece of wire, a 6mm crystal, a
pacer bead, and a 4mm crystal.
ssembly that follows a Saucer
Link is constructed between two
d loops. Following steps 1–5,
g a Wrapped Loop Around a Chain
in one end loop of a Saucer Spacer
the bail on the Crystal Pillow Drop.
wrapped loop on the other end.
an earring finding to the wrapped
ssemble a second earring.

Growing Frida's Flower

I've always had the privilege of sharing my life with dogs. On occasion my sweet greyhound, Frida, would slowly and repeatedly circle a large juniper in my backyard. For years, I thought her behavior was bizarre. Toward the end of Frida's life, I finally understood what was happening: As the branches stroked her body from head to hindquarters, complete contentment registered on her face. Frida showed me the value of living in the present. I pass that idea along to you in this set.

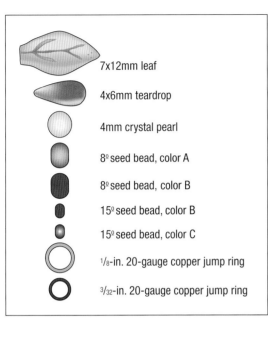

7x12mm leaf

4x6mm teardrop

4mm crystal pearl

8º seed bead, color A

8º seed bead, color B

15º seed bead, color B

15º seed bead, color C

1/8-in. 20-gauge copper jump ring

3/32-in. 20-gauge copper jump ring

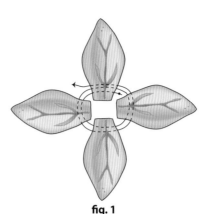

fig. 1

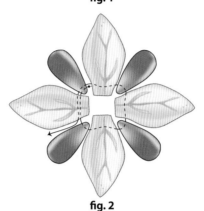

fig. 2

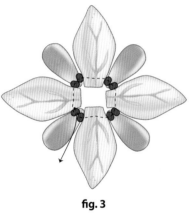

fig. 3

fig. 4

Beadweaving

FLOWER

1 Note: The Flower is stitched with all color-B 8º and color-B 15º seed beads. Thread a needle onto 20 in. of thread, pick up four 7x12mm leaves, and form the beads into a ring by sewing through all four leaves and the first one again, leaving a 6-in. tail [**fig. 1**].

2 Pick up a 4x6mm teardrop bead, and sew through the next leaf. Repeat three times, and step up through the first teardrop picked up in this step and the next leaf [**fig. 2**].

3 Pick up two 15º seed beads, and sew through the next leaf. Repeat three times. On the third repeat, sew through the first 15º picked up in this step [**fig. 3**].

4 Pick up two 15ºs, and sew through the next leaf and the first 15º in the next set of two. Repeat three more times. Step up through the first two 15ºs picked up in this step and the next leaf [**fig. 4**]. To this point, you have been working on the back of the Flower.

Tools & Materials
For all accessories

Tools/supplies
- Fireline 6 lb. test
- Beading needles, #12
- Thread burner
- Scissors
- **2** pairs of chainnose or bentnose pliers (or one of each)
- Grooved looping pliers
- Looping pliers
- Flush cutters
- Ruler

Flower
- **4** 7x12mm leaves (Czech glass, terracotta)
- **4** 4x6mm teardrop beads (Czech glass, green stone finish)
- 4mm pearl (Swarovski 5810, gold)
- Bracelet: **4** 8º seed beads, color B (Toho 502, raspberry bronze metallic)
- Bracelet: **12** 15º seed beads, color B
- Necklace and earrings: **28** 15º seed beads, color B

Arrow
- **4** 8º seed beads , color A (Miyuki 2035, matte metallic khaki iris)
- 8º seed bead, color B
- **4** 15º seed beads, color C (Miyuki 229, teal-lined olive)
- **20** 15º seed beads , color B

Two-Sided Square
- **28** 8º seed beads, color A
- **40** 15º seed beads, color B
- **8** 15º seed beads, color C

Butterfly Link
- 1¾ in. 20-gauge copper wire
- **2** ³⁄₃₂-in. jump rings

Pearl Eyepin Link
- 1 in. 20-gauge copper wire
- 4mm pearl (Swarovski 5810, gold)

Materials for Necklace, Bracelet, and Earrings on page 61

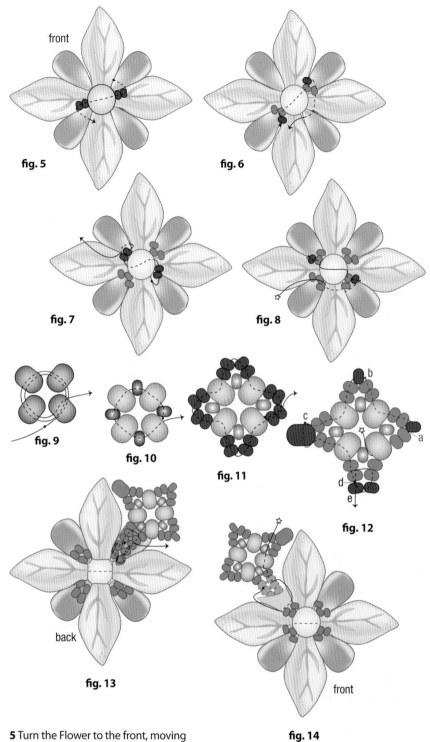

front

fig. 5

fig. 6

fig. 7

fig. 8

fig. 9

fig. 10

fig. 11

fig. 12

b

c

a

d

e

back

fig. 13

front

fig. 14

ARROW

1 Thread a needle onto 20 in. of thread, pick up four color-A 8º seed beads, and form the beads into a ring by sewing through all four As, leaving a 6-in. tail. Step up through the first A [**fig. 9**].

2 Pick up a color-C 15º seed bead, and sew through the next A. Repeat three times, but do not step up at the end of the round [**fig. 10**].

3 Pick up four color-B 15ºs, and sew through the next A. Repeat three times, and step up through the first two B 15ºs picked up in this step [**fig. 11**].

4 Pick up a B 15º, and sew through the next two B 15ºs, the A, and the following two B 15ºs [**fig. 12, a–b**]. Repeat this stitch once [**fig. 12, b–c**]. Pick up a color-B 8º seed bead, and sew through the next two B 15ºs, the A, and the next two B 15ºs [**fig. 12, c–d**]. Pick up two B 15ºs, sew through the two B 15ºs shown, and step up through the first B 15º just picked up [**fig. 12, d–e**]. End the tail, but do not end the working thread. The working thread is used to attach the Arrow to the Flower.

Attaching the Arrows to the Flower
1 With the holes of the pearl aligned horizontally (red dotted line), turn the Flower to the back, position an Arrow, and sew through the beadwork as shown [**fig. 13**]. Reinforce the thread path to secure. Turn the flower to the front. Sew through the teardrop on the flower, and sew back through the Arrow as shown. End the threads [**fig. 14**].

Note: In fig. 14, the teardrop is only partially shown in order to reveal the thread path through the beads in the Arrow that are behind the teardrop.

2 On the back of the Flower, position a second Arrow to the left of the first Arrow. Work as in step 1 to attach the second Arrow on the front of the Flower.

5 Turn the Flower to the front, moving the bottom leaf to the top, and sew through the next teardrop. Pick up two 15ºs, a 4mm pearl, and two 15ºs, and sew through the opposite teardrop [**fig. 5**].

6 Pick up a 15º, and sew through the 15º adjoining the pearl, the pearl and the next 15º. Pick up a 15º, and sew through the next teardrop, leaf, and teardrop [**fig. 6**].

7 Pick up two 15ºs, sew through the next pearl, pick up two 15ºs, and sew through the opposite teardrop [**fig. 7**].

8 Pick up a 15º, and sew through the 15º adjoining the pearl, the pearl and the next 15º. Pick up a 15º. Sew through the next teardrop and leaf. End the threads [**fig. 8**].

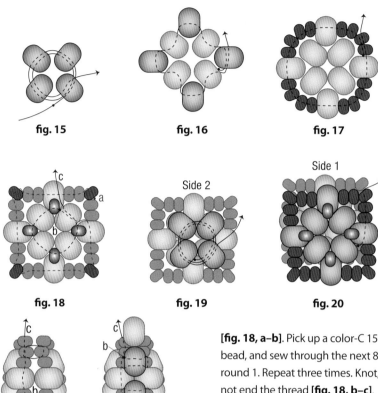

fig. 15   **fig. 16**   **fig. 17**

fig. 18   Side 2 / fig. 19   Side 1 / fig. 20

fig. 21   **fig. 22**

TWO-SIDED SQUARE

1 Round 1: Thread a needle onto 24 in. of thread, pick up four color-A 8º seed beads, and form the beads into a ring by sewing through all four 8ºs, leaving an 8-in. tail. Step up through the first 8º [**fig. 15**].

2 Round 2: Pick up an 8º, and sew through the next 8º. Repeat three times, and step up through the first 8º picked up in this step [**fig. 16**].

3 Round 3: Pick up four color-B 15º seed beads, and sew through the next 8º. Repeat three times, and step up through the first two Bs picked up in this step [**fig. 17**].

4 Pick up a B, and sew through the next two Bs, the 8º, and the following two Bs. Repeat two times. Pick up a B, and sew through the next two Bs, the following 8º in round 2, and the next 8º in round 1

[**fig. 18, a–b**]. Pick up a color-C 15º seed bead, and sew through the next 8º in round 1. Repeat three times. Knot, but do not end the thread [**fig. 18, b–c**].

5 Flip the square over horizontally from right to left. Place a needle on the tail thread. To make the second side of the square, repeat steps 1–4; start round 1 sewing close to the first side [**fig. 19**]. End the thread on side 2. Flip the square over horizontally from left to right. Place a needle on the thread attached to side 1, and sew through the 8º in round 2 and the next three Bs [**fig. 20**].

6 To join the two square sides, pick up an 8º, and sew down through the B on side 2. Sew back through the 8º just picked up, and sew up through the two Bs on side 1 [**fig. 21, a–b**]. Sew through the beadwork as shown to continue joining the sides [**fig. 21, b–c**]. Repeat three times.

7 Sew through the next two Bs, and pick up an 8º. Sew down through the B on side 2, back through the 8º just added, and up through the B, the 8º, and the B on side 1 [**fig. 22, a–b**]. Pick up an 8º, and sew down through the B on side 2. Sew back through the 8º just picked up, and up through the three Bs on side 1 [**fig. 22, b–c**]. Repeat three times, and end the thread.

Materials
For each accessory

Necklace, 18 in.
- Flower
- **2** Arrows
- **6** Two-Sided Squares
- 6 ft. 20-gauge copper wire to make 20 Butterfly Links and 14 Pearl Eyepin Links
- **30** ⅛-in. 20-gauge copper jump rings
- **78** ³⁄₃₂-in. 20-gauge copper jump rings
- 15mm square/27mm bar hammered copper toggle clasp

Bracelet, 7½ in.
- Flower
- **4** Two-Sided Squares
- **46** 8º seed beads, color B
- Gram 15º seed beads, color B
- 2 ft. 20-gauge copper wire to make 6 Butterfly Links and 8 Pearl Eyepin Links
- **24** ⅛-in. 20-gauge copper jump rings
- **20** ³⁄₃₂-in. 20-gauge copper jump rings
- 15mm square/27mm bar hammered copper toggle clasp

Earrings, 1⅝ in.
- **2** Flowers
- **4** Arrows
- 5 in. 20-gauge copper wire to make 2 Butterfly Links
- **6** ⅛-in. 20-gauge copper jump rings
- **4** ³⁄₃₂-in. 20-gauge copper jump rings
- Pair of copper earring findings

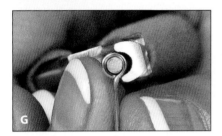
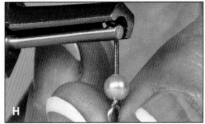

Wirework

BUTTERFLY LINK

1 A Butterfly Link is made up of two wire wings joined with jump rings. To make a wing, cut ⅞ in. of wire, and make a P-shaped Loop following "Making a P-shaped loop with grooved looping pliers" (p. 20), working in the second groove of the pliers.

2 Holding the first loop between your left thumb and forefinger, repeat on the other end of the wire **[A]**.

3 Repeat steps 1 and 2 to make a second wing. Join the wings by threading a ³/₃₂-in. jump ring through one pair of loops **[B]** and repeat with another ³/₃₂-in. jump ring to join the remaining pair of loops.

PEARL EYEPIN LINK

1 Cut 1 in. of wire. Place the wire in the jaws of the grooved looping pliers so the wire end is even with the end of the jaw **[C]**.

2 Close the jaws **[D]**. Round the end of the wire a bit more, and continue to rotate to make a closed circle **[E]**.

3 Place the end of the curved jaw at the point where the wires meet **[F]**. Brace the wire end with your left forefinger. Squeeze the jaws and rotate the pliers back toward you, so the loop is centered in the middle of the wire **[G]**. This is referred to as "breaking the neck."

4 Slide a 4mm pearl on the wire so it rests against the first loop. Hold the bead by the loop so the side of the loop where the ends meet is facing you. To make the second loop, place the wire into the jaws of the grooved looping pliers, making sure the end of the wire is even with the end of the jaw. Squeeze the jaws to make the first bend **[H]**. Round the end of the wire a little bit more, and continue to rotate to make a closed circle **[I]**. Break the neck **[J]**. Check the roundness of the loop. Reinsert the pliers and adjust as needed.

Accessories

NECKLACE
Setup

1 Make one Flower following steps 1–8 of "Flower."

2 Make two Arrows following steps 1–4 of "Arrow."

3 Attach the Arrows to the Flower followings steps 1 and 2 of "Attaching the Arrows to the Flower."

4 Make six Two-Sided Squares following steps 1–7 of "Two-Sided Square."

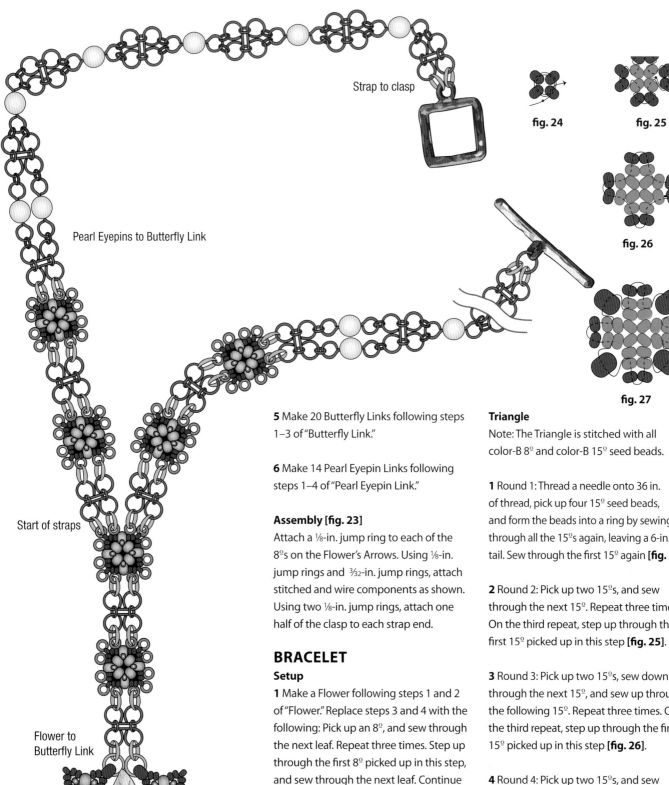

Strap to clasp

Pearl Eyepins to Butterfly Link

Start of straps

Flower to
Butterfly Link

fig. 23

fig. 24

fig. 25

fig. 26

fig. 27

5 Make 20 Butterfly Links following steps 1–3 of "Butterfly Link."

6 Make 14 Pearl Eyepin Links following steps 1–4 of "Pearl Eyepin Link."

Assembly [fig. 23]

Attach a ⅛-in. jump ring to each of the 8ºs on the Flower's Arrows. Using ⅛-in. jump rings and ³⁄₃₂-in. jump rings, attach stitched and wire components as shown. Using two ⅛-in. jump rings, attach one half of the clasp to each strap end.

BRACELET
Setup

1 Make a Flower following steps 1 and 2 of "Flower." Replace steps 3 and 4 with the following: Pick up an 8º, and sew through the next leaf. Repeat three times. Step up through the first 8º picked up in this step, and sew through the next leaf. Continue with steps 5–8.

2 Make four Two-Sided Squares following steps 1–7 of "Two-Sided Square."

3 Make six Butterfly Links following steps 1–3 of "Butterfly Link."

4 Make eight Pearl Eyepin Links following steps 1–4 of "Pearl Eyepin Link."

Triangle

Note: The Triangle is stitched with all color-B 8º and color-B 15º seed beads.

1 Round 1: Thread a needle onto 36 in. of thread, pick up four 15º seed beads, and form the beads into a ring by sewing through all the 15ºs again, leaving a 6-in. tail. Sew through the first 15º again [fig. 24].

2 Round 2: Pick up two 15ºs, and sew through the next 15º. Repeat three times. On the third repeat, step up through the first 15º picked up in this step [fig. 25].

3 Round 3: Pick up two 15ºs, sew down through the next 15º, and sew up through the following 15º. Repeat three times. On the third repeat, step up through the first 15º picked up in this step [fig. 26].

4 Round 4: Pick up two 15ºs, and sew down through the next 15º. Pick up an 8º, and sew up through the next 15º. Repeat three times. On the third repeat, step up through the first 15º picked up in this step [fig. 27].

5 Round 5: Pick up two 15ºs, and sew down through the next 15º. Pick up a 15º, and sew through the next 8º. Pick up a 15º, and sew up through the next 15º. Repeat three times. On the third repeat,

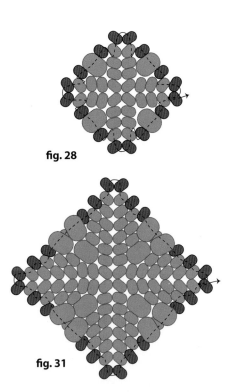

fig. 28

fig. 29

fig. 30

fig. 31

fig. 32

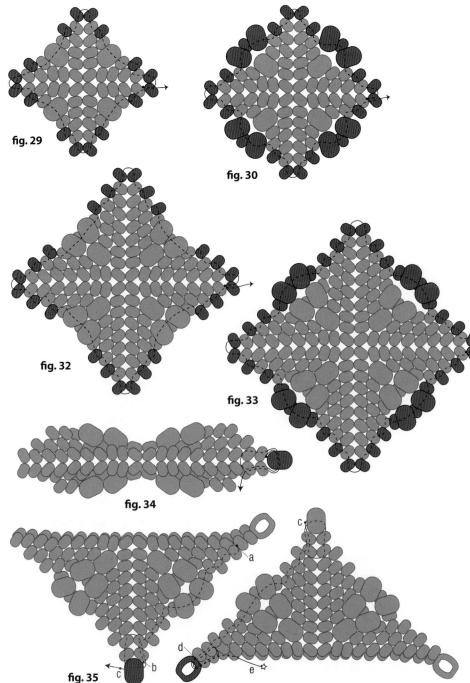

fig. 33

fig. 34

fig. 35

step up through the first 15º picked up in this step [**fig. 28**].

6 Round 6: Pick up two 15ºs, and sew down through the next 15º. Pick up a 15º. Sew through the next 15º, 8º, and 15º. Pick up a 15º, and sew up through the next 15º. Repeat three times. On the third repeat, step up through the first 15º picked up in this step [**fig. 29**].

7 Round 7: Pick up two 15ºs, and sew down through the next 15º. Pick up a 15º, and sew through the next 15º. Pick up an 8º, a 15º, and an 8º, and sew through the next 15º. Pick up a 15º, and sew up through the next 15º. Repeat three times. On the third repeat, step up through the first 15º picked up in this step [**fig. 30**]. The Triangle will start to bow and curve.

8 Round 8: Pick up two 15ºs, and sew down through the next 15º. Pick up a 15º, and sew through the next 15º. Pick up a 15º, and sew through the next 8º, 15º, and 8º. Pick up a 15º, and sew through the next 15º. Pick up a 15º, and sew up through the next 15º. Repeat three times. On the third repeat, step up through the first 15º picked up in this step [**fig. 31**].

9 Round 9: Pick up two 15ºs, and sew down through the next 15º. Pick up a 15º, and sew through the next 15º in round 8. Pick up a 15º, and sew through the next five beads. Pick up a 15º, and sew through the next 15º. Pick up a 15º, and sew up through the next 15º. Repeat three times. On the third repeat, step up through the first 15º picked up in this step [**fig. 32**].

10 Round 10: Pick up two 15ºs, and sew down through the next 15º. Pick up a 15º, and sew through the next 15º. Pick up a

15º, and sew through the next 15º. Pick up a 15º, an 8º, a 15º, an 8º, and a 15º, and sew through the next 15º. Pick up a 15º, and sew through the next 15º. Pick up a 15º, and sew up through the next 15º. Repeat three times. On the third repeat, step up through the first 15º picked up in this step [**fig. 33**].

11 Fold the beadwork in half to form a Triangle. With the fold facing you, pick up an 8º, and sew through the next two 15ºs as shown [**fig. 34**].

64

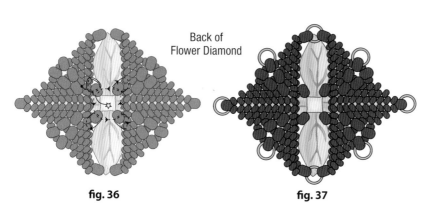

fig. 36   Back of Flower Diamond   **fig. 37**

12 Sew though the beadwork as shown to exit a 15° in the opposite corner [**fig. 35, a–b**]. Pick up an 8°, and sew up through the next two 15°s [**fig. 35, b–c**]. Turn the Triangle over. Sew down through the 15° that corresponds to the 15° the thread is exiting. Sew across and down through the 15° on the corner to the right of the 8° picked up in **b–c**. Sew through the 8° and the beadwork to exit a 15° in the opposite corner [**fig. 35, c–d**]. Pick up an 8°, sew through the next two 15°s as shown, and end both threads [**fig. 35, d–e**].

13 Repeat steps 1–12 to make a second Triangle.

Flower Diamond

1 To make a Flower Diamond, add thread to a Triangle at the start point, and sew through the beadwork as shown [**fig. 36**]. End the thread.

2 Attach eight ⅛-in. jump rings to the 8°s in the Flower Diamond as shown [**fig. 37**]. On the front of the Flower Diamond, attach a Pearl Eyepin Link to each jump ring [**fig. 38**].

Assembly

Use ⅛-in. jump rings to attach stitched and wire components. Use ³⁄₃₂-in. jump rings to attach one half of the clasp to each end Butterfly Link [**fig. 39**].

fig. 38

EARRINGS

Setup

1 Make two Flowers following steps 1–8 of "Flower."

2 Make four Arrows following steps 1–4 of "Arrow."

3 Attach the Arrows to the Flower following steps 1 and 2 of "Attaching the Arrows to the Flower."

4 Make two Butterfly Links following steps 1–3 of "Butterfly Link."

Assembly [fig. 40]

Attach a jump ring to each of the 8°s on the Arrows, but before closing each jump ring, attach the bottom wing of a Butterfly Link. Attach a jump ring through the top wing of the Butterfly Link and to an earring finding. Assemble a second earring.

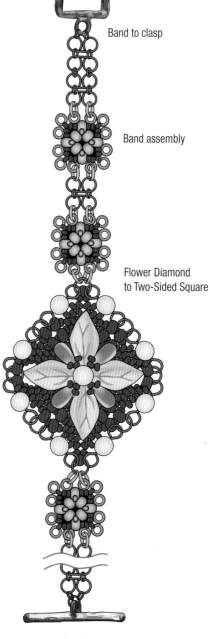

Band to clasp

Band assembly

Flower Diamond to Two-Sided Square

fig. 39

fig. 40

Simply Divine

This set is a blissful expression of life in beads and wire. Each time I drape the lariat around my neck, I smile, preen a little bit, and think, "This is just divine!"

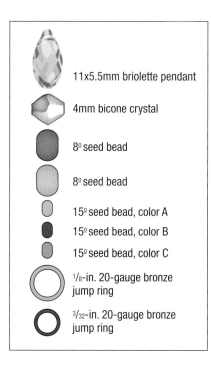

11x5.5mm briolette pendant

4mm bicone crystal

8º seed bead

8º seed bead

15º seed bead, color A

15º seed bead, color B

15º seed bead, color C

1/8-in. 20-gauge bronze jump ring

3/32-in. 20-gauge bronze jump ring

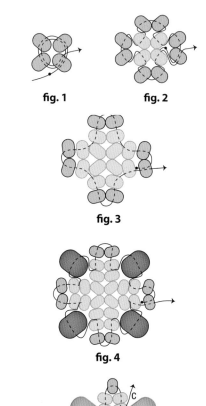

fig. 1

fig. 2

fig. 3

fig. 4

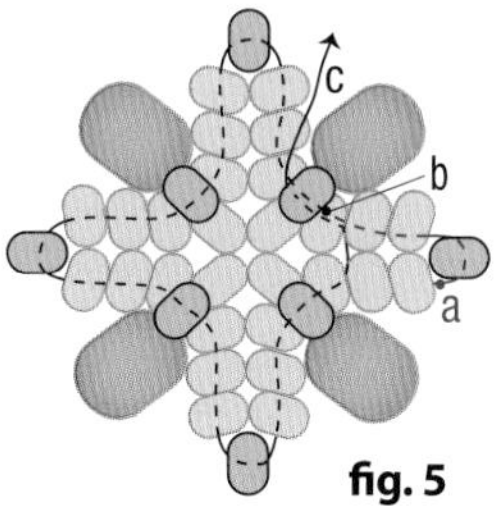

fig. 5

Beadweaving

CRYSTAL HERRINGBONE COMPONENT

Single-Sided

1 Round 1: Thread a needle onto 24 in. of thread, pick up four 15º seed beads, and form the beads into a ring by sewing through all four beads again, leaving a 6-in. tail [**fig. 1**]. Step up through the first 15º.

2 Round 2: Pick up two 15ºs, and sew through the next 15º. Repeat three times, and step up through the first 15º picked up in this step [**fig. 2**].

3 Round 3: Pick up two 15ºs, sew down through the next 15º in the previous round, and sew up through the following 15º. Repeat three times, and step up through the first 15º picked up in this step [**fig. 3**].

4 Round 4: Pick up two 15ºs, and sew down through the next 15º in the previous round. Pick up an 8º seed bead, and sew up through the next 15º. Repeat three times, and step up through the first 15º picked up in this step [**fig. 4**].

5 Round 5: Pick up a 15º (this bead forms a point at the end of round 4), and sew down through the next three 15ºs in rounds 4, 3, and 2 [**fig. 5, a–b**]. Pick up a 15º (this 15º starts the raised portion of the component and sits at an angle between each 15º in round 2), and sew up through the next three 15ºs in rounds 2, 3, and 4. Starting with **a–b**, repeat three more times, making this change to the third repeat: After picking up the raised 15º, sew through the adjacent 15ºs in round 2, and step up through the first raised 15º picked up in this step [**fig. 5, b–c**].

Tools & Materials
For all accessories

Tools/supplies
- Fireline 6 lb. test
- Beading needles, #12
- Thread burner
- Scissors
- **2** pairs of chainnose or bentnose pliers (or one of each)
- Grooved looping pliers
- Flush cutters
- Ruler

Single-Sided Crystal Herringbone Component
- 4mm bicone crystal (Swarovski 5328, peridot satin)
- **4** 8º seed beads (Miyuki 2067, silvery green matte metallic iris)
- **44** 15º seed beads (Toho 952, rainbow light topaz seafoam-lined)

Double-Sided Crystal Herringbone Component
- **2** 4mm bicone crystals (Swarovski 5328, peridot satin)
- **4** 8º seed beads (Miyuki 2067, silvery green matte metallic iris)
- **84** 15º seed beads (Toho 952, rainbow light topaz seafoam-lined)

Netted Tube
- **2** 8º seed beads (Matsuno 356F, teal-lined topaz)
- **18** 15º seed beads (Toho 952, rainbow light topaz seafoam-lined), color A
- **68–104** 15º seed beads (Miyuki 502 3-cut, raspberry bronze metallic), color B
- **48–66** 15º seed beads (Toho 203, amethyst rose gold luster), color C

Materials for Necklace, Bracelet, and Earrings on page 69

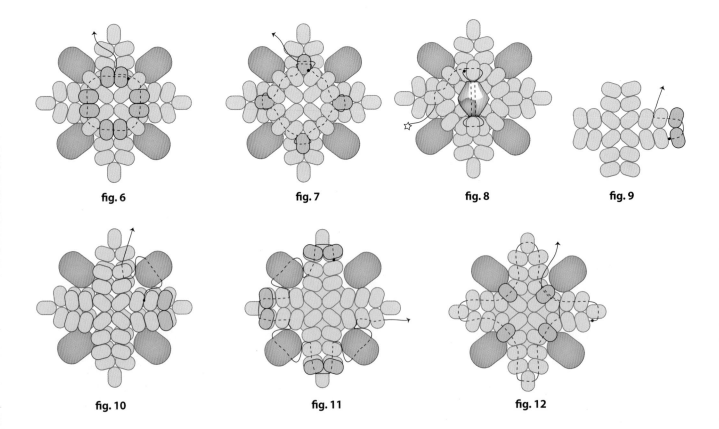

fig. 6   fig. 7   fig. 8   fig. 9

fig. 10   fig. 11   fig. 12

6 Pick up two 15ºs, and sew through the next raised 15º. Repeat three times, and step up through the first 15º picked up in this step [**fig. 6**].

7 Pick up a 15º, and sew through the next three raised 15ºs. Repeat three times, and step up through the first 15º picked up in this step [**fig. 7**].

8 Pick up a 4mm bicone crystal, and sew through the 15º opposite the one your thread is exiting. Sew back through the 4mm and the 15º your thread exited at the start of this step. End the working thread and tail [**fig. 8**].

Double-Sided

1 Make one Single-Sided Crystal Herringbone Component following steps 1–8 of "Crystal Herringbone Component, Single-Sided." Set the component aside.

2 Follow steps 1–3 of "Crystal Herringbone Component, Single-Sided." End the tail thread. With the working thread, pick up two 15ºs, and sew through the next 15º in the previous round [**fig. 9**]. Place

the Crystal Herringbone Component completed in step 1 against the back of the component in progress. To join: Sew through the 8º on the completed component, and sew up through the next 15º in round 3 of the component in progress [**fig. 10**]. Pick up two 15ºs, and sew through the next 15º in the previous round of the component in progress. Sew through the 8º on the completed component, and sew up through the next 15º in round 3 of the component in progress. Repeat two more times, and step up through the first 15º picked up this step [**fig. 11**].

3 Without picking up any beads, sew through a 15º that forms a point on the completed component. Continue through the adjacent 15ºs in rounds 4, 3, and 2 of the component in progress. Pick up a 15º, and sew up through the next three 15ºs in rounds 2, 3, and 4. Repeat three more times, making this change to the third repeat: After picking up the raised 15º, sew through the adjacent 15º in round 2, and step up through the first 15º picked up in this step [**fig. 12**].

4 Follow steps 6–8 of "Crystal Herringbone Component, Single-Sided." Before adding the 4mm crystal in step 8, check that it sits at the same orientation as the crystal on side 1. If not, advance to the next raised point and add the crystal. End the thread.

NETTED TUBE

1 Thread a needle onto 36 in. of thread, pick up three color-B 15º seed beads, and form the beads into a ring by sewing through all three Bs, leaving a 12-in. tail. Step up through the first B [**fig. 13**]. This is the base round from which the netted and peyote rounds are built.

2 Pick up a B, a color-C 15º seed bead, and a B, and sew through the next B in the previous round. Repeat two times, and step up through the first B and C picked up in this step [**fig. 14**].

3 Pick up a B, a C, and a B, and sew through the next C in the previous round. Repeat two times, and step up through the first B and C picked up in this step [**fig. 15**].

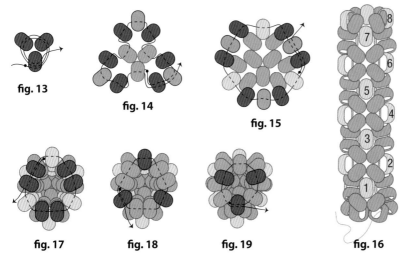

fig. 13

fig. 14

fig. 15

fig. 17

fig. 18

fig. 19

fig. 16

4 Repeat step 3 six more times to complete a total of eight netted rounds. To count the number of netted rounds, pinch the tube to flatten it, and count the Cs as shown, starting from the bottom [**fig. 16**].

5 Using tubular peyote stitch, begin to narrow the tube with this round: Pick up two Bs, and sew through the next C in the previous round. Repeat two more times, and step up through the first two Bs picked up in this step [**fig. 17**].

6 Pick up a B, and sew through the next two Bs in the previous round. Repeat two more times, and step up through the first B picked up in this round [**fig. 18**].

7 Pick up a B, and sew through the next B in the previous round. Repeat two more times, and step up through the first B picked up in this round [**fig. 19**].

8 Stitch four peyote rounds using Cs.

9 Stitch three peyote rounds using color-A 15° seed beads.

10 Pick up an 8° seed bead, and sew through the two As in rounds 2 and 3 from left to right [**fig. 20, a–b**]. Sew through the 8° in the same direction [**fig. 20, b–c**].

11 To join: Sew though the two As in rounds 2 and 3 from left to right and end the working thread [**fig. 21**].

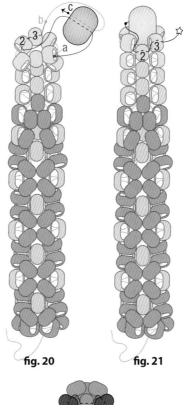

fig. 20

fig. 21

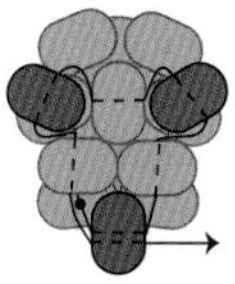

fig. 22

12 Thread a needle on the tail, pick up a B, and sew through the next B. Repeat two more times, and step up through the first B picked up in this step [**fig. 22**]. This is a peyote round worked off the base round noted in step 1.

13 Repeat steps 8–10 to complete the Netted Tube.

Materials
For each accessory

Necklace, 28 in.
- **11** Single-Sided Crystal Components
- **17** Netted Tubes (1 14-Round and 16 8-Round)
- **44** ⅛-in. 20-gauge bronze jump rings
- **78** ³⁄₃₂-in. 20-gauge bronze jump rings
- 5 ft. 20-gauge bronze craft wire to make 37 S-Links
- 11x5.5mm briolette pendant (Swarovski 6010, peridot)

Bracelet, 7½ in.
- **6** Single-Sided Crystal Components
- **24** ⅛-in. 20-gauge bronze jump rings
- **38** ³⁄₃₂-in. 20-gauge bronze jump rings
- 2 ft. 20-gauge bronze craft wire to make 12 S-Links, S-Hook, and Eye Clasp

Earrings, 1½ in.
- **2** Double-Sided Crystal Herringbone Components
- **4** Netted Tubes
- **10** ⅛-in. 20-gauge bronze jump rings
- **12** ³⁄₃₂-in. 20-gauge bronze jump rings
- 5 in. 20-gauge bronze craft wire to make 4 S-Links
- Pair of copper earring findings

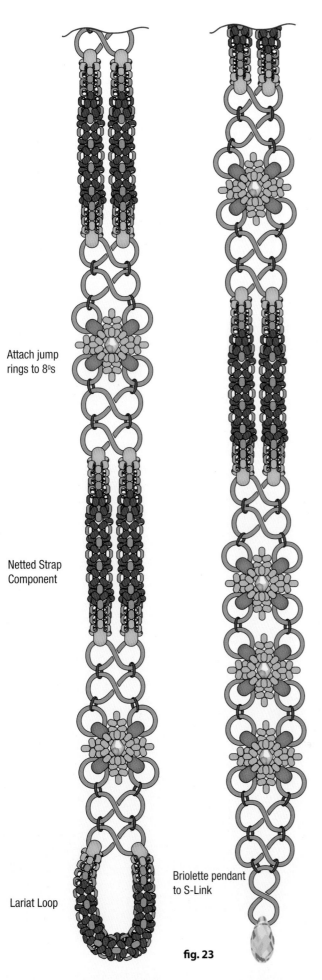

Attach jump rings to 8ºs

Netted Strap Component

Lariat Loop

Briolette pendant to S-Link

fig. 23

Wirework

S-LINK

1 Cut 1⅛ in. of wire. Working in the third groove of the looping pliers, create a P-shaped loop following "Making a P-shaped loop with grooved looping pliers" (p. 20).

2 Repeat on the other end of the wire, but make the P shape in the opposite direction **[A]**.

Accessories

NECKLACE

Setup

1 Make 11 Single-Sided Crystal Herringbone Components following steps 1–8 of "Crystal Herringbone Component, Single-Sided."

2 Make 16 Netted Tubes following steps 1–13 of "Netted Tube." Make one Netted Tube following steps 1–3 and 5–13 of "Netted Tube", but after completing step 3, repeat step 3 12 more times to make a total of 14 netted rounds. This is a 14-Round Netted Tube.

3 Make 37 S-Links following steps 1 and 2 of "S-Link."

Assembly [fig. 23]

Attach a ⅛-in. jump ring to each 8º in the 11 Crystal Herringbone Components. Build eight Netted Strap Components by attaching pairs of Netted Tubes with an S-Link on each end. Attach both ends of an S-Link to the 14-Round Netted Tube to form the Lariat Loop. Attach the briolette pendant to an S-Link. Using ³⁄₃₂-in. jump rings, attach the remaining stitched and wire components to complete the necklace assembly as shown.

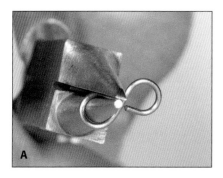

A

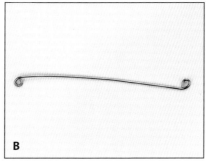

B

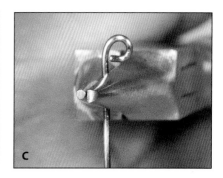

C

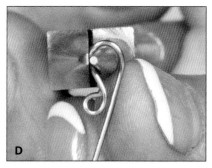

D

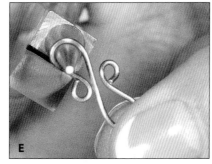

E

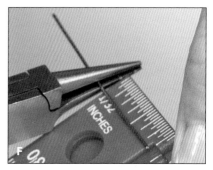

F

BRACELET

Setup

1 Make six Single-Sided Crystal Herringbone Components following steps 1–8 of "Crystal Herringbone Component, Single-Sided."

2 Make 12 S-Links following steps 1 and 2 of "S-Link" **[A]**.

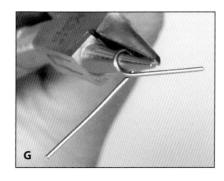

G

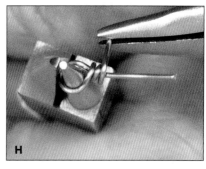

H

S-Hook and Eye Clasp

1 To make an S-Hook, cut 2 in. of wire. Working in the first groove of the grooved looping pliers, create a P-shaped loop following "Making a P-shaped loop." Repeat on the other end of the wire, but make the P shape in the opposite direction **[B]**.

2 Position the wire in the third groove directly under one of the loops, with the P shape facing you **[C]**.

3 Bracing the wire with your left thumb, roll the pliers away from you until the P touches the straight wire **[D]**. Holding the half just completed between your thumb and forefinger, repeat on the other end of the wire **[E]**.

4 To make an Eye Clasp, cut 2 in. of wire. Position the wire in the third groove, approximately ⅞ in. from the end **[F]**. Wrap the other end of the wire around the pliers to form the eye **[G]**. Reposition the eye in the pliers, and wrap the long end three or four times around the short end **[H]**. Roll the pliers toward you to center the eye on the wire. Flush-cut the coil, and use bentnose or chainnose pliers to press in the coil end.

5 Position the wire end in the first groove, and make the end loop **[I]**.

I

Assembly [fig. 24]

Attach a ⅛-in. jump ring to each corner 8º in the six Crystal Herringbone Components. Using ³⁄₃₂-in. jump rings, attach all the components. After attaching the S-Hook, use your fingers to gently squeeze the attached loop to meet the wire's center [**fig. 24**].

EARRINGS

Setup

1 Make two Double-Sided Crystal Herringbone Components following steps 1–4 of "Crystal Herringbone Component, Double-Sided."

2 Make four Netted Tubes following steps 1–13 of "Netted Tube."

3 Using a ⅞-in. piece of wire with the end positioned in the second groove of the looping pliers, make four S-Links following steps 1 and 2 of "S-Links."

Assembly

1 Using a ⅛-in. jump ring, attach one end of a Netted Tube to the upper left corner 8º on a Double-Sided Crystal Herringbone Component. Using a ⅛-in. jump ring, attach the other end of the Netted Tube to the lower right corner 8º [**fig. 25**].

2 Repeat to attach a second Netted Tube to the opposite corner 8ºs. Using six ³⁄₃₂-in. jump rings, attach the other components as shown. Attach an earring finding to the ⅛-in. jump ring [**fig. 26**]. Assemble a second earring.

fig. 24

fig. 25

fig. 26

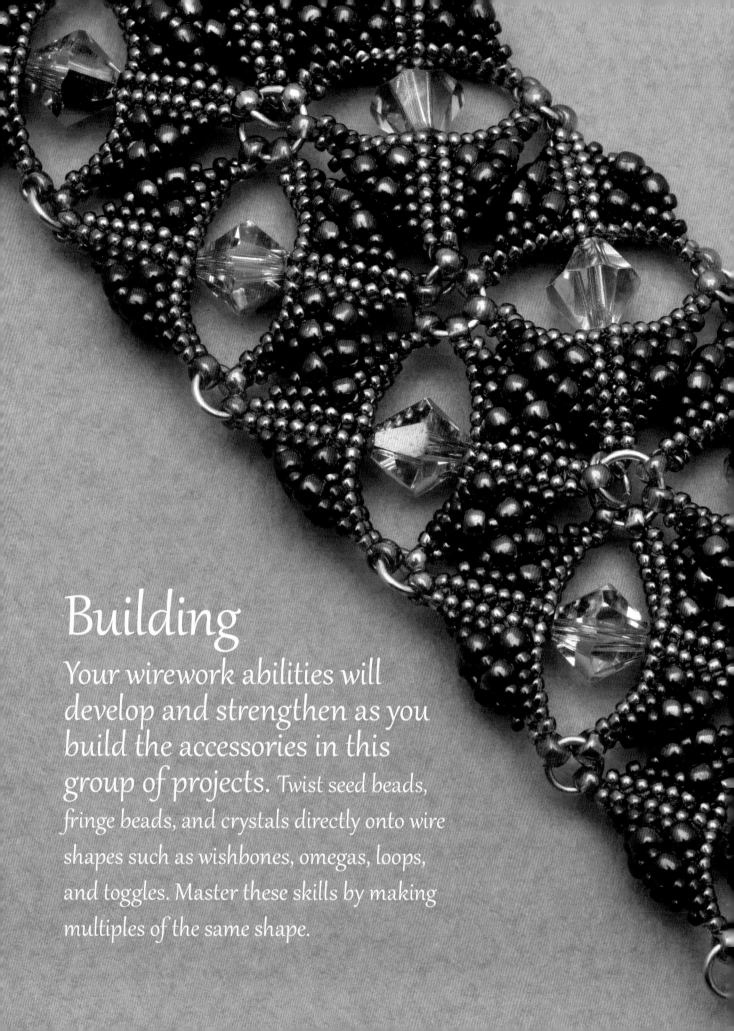

Building

Your wirework abilities will develop and strengthen as you build the accessories in this group of projects. Twist seed beads, fringe beads, and crystals directly onto wire shapes such as wishbones, omegas, loops, and toggles. Master these skills by making multiples of the same shape.

In Buttons and Bowls

"Let's go where I'll keep on wearin' those frills and flowers and buttons and bows." These are lyrics from "In Buttons and Bows", a popular song from the 1940s. I found myself singing this lyric over and over as I was making this set. I promise you'll stand out in pretty stitched Buttons and frilly stitched Bowls (please pardon the pun).

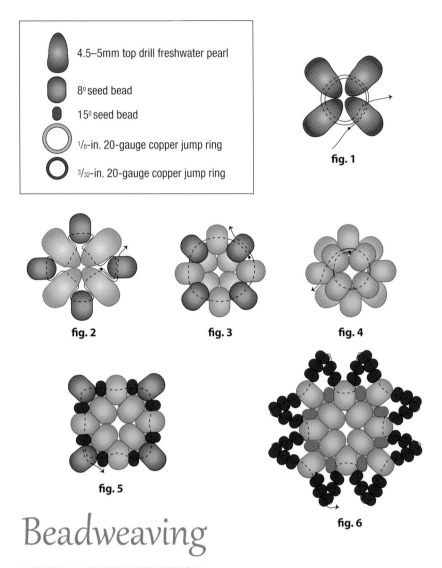

fig. 1

fig. 2

fig. 3

fig. 4

fig. 5

fig. 6

Tools & Materials
For all accessories

Tools/supplies
- Fireline 6 lb. test (crystal)
- Beading needles, #12
- Thread burner
- Scissors
- **2** pairs of chainnose or bentnose pliers (or one of each)
- Grooved looping pliers
- Flush cutters
- Ruler

Bowl Link and Pendant Bowl Link
- **4** 4.5-5mm top-drilled fuchsia freshwater pearls
- **14–15** 8º seed beads (Matsuno F650, rainbow green silver-lined matte)
- **80** 15º seed beads (Toho 703, raspberry bronze matte)

Pearl Button
- **4** 4.5–5mm top-drilled fuchsia freshwater pearls
- **12** 8º seed beads (Matsuno F650, rainbow green silver-lined matte)
- **8** 15º seed beads (Toho 703, raspberry bronze matte)

Freestanding Omega Link, Attached Omega Link, Freestanding Wishbone Link, or Attached Wishbone Link
- **2** 8º seed beads (Matsuno F650, rainbow green silver-lined matte)
- 1⁵⁄₁₆ in. 20-gauge copper wire

Materials for Necklace, Bracelet, and Earrings on page 77

Beadweaving

BOWL LINK FOUNDATION

1 Round 1: Thread a needle onto 30 in. of thread, pick up four 4.5–5mm top-drilled pearls, and form the beads into a ring by sewing through all four pearls again, leaving a 6-in. tail. Step up through the first pearl [**fig. 1**].

2 Round 2: Pick up an 8º seed bead and sew through the next pearl. Repeat three times, and step up through the first 8º picked up in this step [**fig. 2**].

3 Round 3: Pick up an 8º and sew through the next 8º in the previous round. Repeat three times, and step up through the first 8º picked up in this step [**fig. 3**]. Sew through the four beads picked up in round 3 and the first one again, so round 3 sits on top of round 1. Step down to the nearest 8º in round 2 [**fig. 4**].

4 Round 4: Pick up a 15º seed bead, an 8º, and a 15º, and sew through the next 8º in round 2. Repeat three times, and step up through the first 15º and 8º picked up in this step [**fig. 5**]. This completes a Pearl Button.

5 Round 5: Pick up five 15ºs, and sew through the next 8º in round 2. Pick up five 15ºs, and sew through the next 8º in round 4. Repeat these two stitches three times, and step up through the first three 15ºs picked up in this step [**fig. 6**].

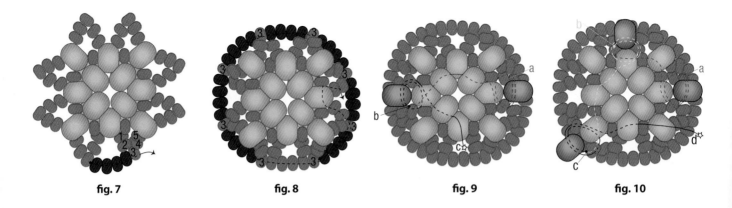

fig. 7   **fig. 8**   **fig. 9**   **fig. 10**

6 Pick up four 15°s, and sew through the third bead in the next five-bead set in round 5 [**fig. 7**]. As you pick up beads, the beadwork will form a bowl shape. Repeat this stitch seven times. To exit, sew through the beadwork as shown [**fig. 8**].

BOWL LINK

1 Follow steps 1–6 of "Bowl Link Foundation."

2 Pick up an 8°, and sew through the beadwork as shown [**fig. 9, a–b**]. Pick up an 8°, and sew through the beadwork as shown [**fig. 9, b–c**]. End the threads.

PENDANT BOWL LINK

1 Follow steps 1–6 of "Bowl Link Foundation."

2 Pick up an 8°, and sew through the beadwork as shown [**fig. 10, a–b**]. Pick up an 8°, and sew through the beadwork as shown [**fig. 10, b–c**]. Pick up an 8°, and sew through the beadwork as shown [**fig. 10, c–d**]. End the threads.

PEARL BUTTON

Complete steps 1–4 of "Bowl Link Foundation." At the end of step 4, sew back through round 4 to reinforce the button. End the threads.

Wirework

FREESTANDING LINK START

Cut 1⁵⁄₁₆ in. of wire. Center the wire in the second groove of the grooved looping pliers. With your fingers, bend the wire around the round jaw, crossing the ends one over the other. As you bend, make sure that even lengths of wire remain on both ends [**A**].

FREESTANDING OMEGA LINK

1 Follow "Freestanding Link Start."

2 String an 8° onto one end of the wire so it butts up against the end of the loop. Position a wire end in the first groove of the grooved looping pliers. Roll the end of the wire up and in to form a closed loop [**B**]. Repeat on the other side [**C**].

FREESTANDING WISHBONE LINK

1 Follow "Freestanding Link Start."

2 Slide an 8° onto one end of the wire so it butts up against the end of the loop. Position a wire end in the first groove of the grooved looping pliers. Roll the end of the wire down and in to form a closed loop [**D**]. Repeat on the other side [**E**].

ATTACHED LINK START

1 Cut 1⁵⁄₁₆ in. of wire. Center the wire in the second groove of the grooved looping pliers. Use your fingers to bend the wire into a U shape [**F**].

2 Pick up the desired component (a button or a bowl). Place the wire through the desired 8° on the component. Center the wire so the bottom of the U sits in the 8° [**G**].

3 With your fingers, hold onto both ends of the U-shaped wire and cross them over one another. As you bend, make sure that even lengths of wire remain on both ends [**H**].

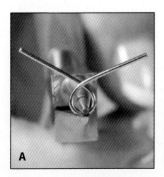
A

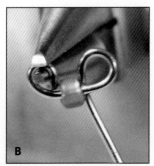
B

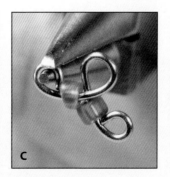
C

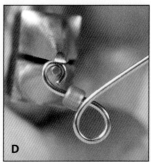
D

ATTACHED OMEGA LINK

1 Follow steps 1–3 of "Attached Link Start."

2 String an 8º onto one end of the wire so it butts up against the end of the loop. Position a wire end in the first groove of the looping pliers. Roll the end of the wire up and in to form a closed loop **[I]**. Repeat on the other side **[J]**.

ATTACHED WISHBONE LINK

1 Follow steps 1–3 of "Attached Link Start."

2 String an 8º onto one end of the wire so it butts up against the end of the loop. Position a wire end in the first groove of the looping pliers. Roll the end of the wire down and in to form a closed loop **[K]**. Repeat on the other side **[L]**.

Materials
For each accessory

Necklace, 18 in.
- **14** Bowl Links
- Pendant Bowl Link
- Pearl Button
- 8 ft. 20-gauge copper wire to make 33 Attached Omega Links, 22 Freestanding Omega Links, and Freestanding Wishbone Link
- **63** ⅛-in. 20-gauge copper jump rings
- 19.5x14mm ring/28mm bar hammered copper toggle clasp

Bracelet, 7 in.
- **11** Pearl Buttons
- 6 ft. 20-gauge copper wire to make 18 Attached Omega Links, 4 Attached Wishbone Links, and 20 Freestanding Wishbone Links
- **82** ⅛-in. 20-gauge copper jump rings
- 4-strand copper tube slide clasp

Earrings, 2 in.
- **2** Bowl Links
- 10 in. 20-gauge copper wire to make 4 Attached Wishbone Links and 2 Freestanding Wishbone Links
- **10** 3/32-in. 20-gauge copper jump rings
- Pair of copper earring findings

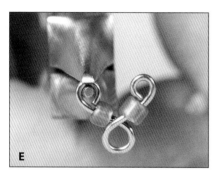

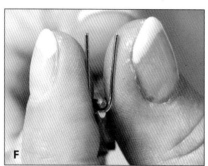

Accessories

NECKLACE

Setup

1 Make 14 Bowl Links following steps 1 and 2 of "Bowl Link." Attach an Omega Link to each of the two 8°s on the back of each Bowl Link following steps 1 and 2 of "Attached Omega Link" [**fig. 11**].

2 Make one Pendant Bowl Link following steps 1 and 2 of "Pendant Bowl Link." Attach an Omega Link to each of the three 8°s on the back the Pendant Bowl Link following steps 1 and 2 of "Attached Omega Link" [**fig. 12**].

3 Make 22 Freestanding Omega Links following steps 1 and 2 of "Freestanding Omega Link."

4 Make one Pearl Button following "Pearl Button." Attach an Omega Link to two 8°s opposite each other in round 4 following steps 1 and 2 of "Attached Omega Link."

5 Make one Freestanding Wishbone Link following steps 1 and 2 of "Freestanding Wishbone Link", but do not add the 8°s in step 2.

Strap to clasp

Bowl Link

Pendant Bowl Link

Pearl Button

fig. 13

fig. 11

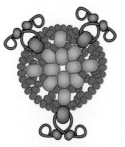

fig. 12

Assembly [fig. 13]

Using jump rings, join the stitched and wire components. Attach one half of the clasp to each end of the strap as shown.

BRACELET

Setup

1 Make 11 Pearl Buttons following "Pearl Button."

2 On seven Pearl Buttons, attach an Omega Link to two 8° seed beads opposite each other in round 4, following steps 1 and 2 of "Attached Omega Link."

3 On four Pearl Buttons, attach an Omega Link to one 8° in round 4, following steps 1 and 2 of "Attached Omega Link." On the same four Pearl Buttons, attach a Wishbone Link to the opposite 8° in round 4, following steps 1 and 2 of "Attached Wishbone Link."

4 Make 20 Freestanding Wishbone Links following steps 1 and 2 of "Freestanding Wishbone Link."

Assembly [fig. 14]

Position two Pearl Buttons with an Attached Omega Link on one end and an Attached Wishbone Link on the other end at either end of the bracelet band. Using four jump rings, connect the Attached Wishbone Links to the clasp. Using two jump rings, attach a Freestanding Wishbone Link to the two center rings of the clasp. Repeat on the other end. Build the bracelet band using jump rings to connect the Pearl Buttons and Freestanding Wishbone Links as shown.

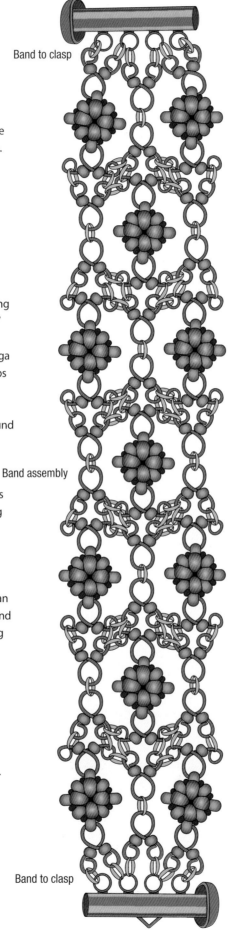

Band to clasp

Band assembly

Band to clasp

fig. 14

fig. 15

EARRINGS

Setup

1 Make two Bowl Links following steps 1 and 2 of "Bowl Link." Attach a Wishbone Link to the two 8°s opposite each other on the back of each Bowl Link, following steps 1 and 2 of "Attached Wishbone Link."

2 Make two Freestanding Wishbone Links following steps 1 and 2 of "Freestanding Wishbone Link", but do not add the 8°s in step 2.

Assembly [fig. 15]

Using jump rings, join the components and attach an earring finding. Assemble a second earring.

A Star Is Born

This composition is drawn together through a mastery of needle, thread, and an ever-increasing skill with pliers. Aurora borealis aqua drop beads accent now-familiar wire Wishbones in curvy comfort.

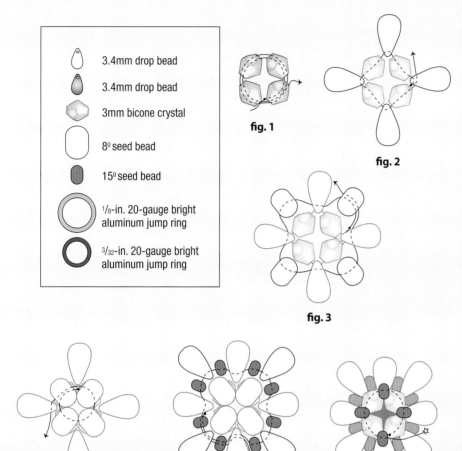

○	3.4mm drop bead
◗	3.4mm drop bead
⬡	3mm bicone crystal
○	8º seed bead
●	15º seed bead
◯	1/8-in. 20-gauge bright aluminum jump ring
◯	3/32-in. 20-gauge bright aluminum jump ring

fig. 1

fig. 2

fig. 3

fig. 4

fig. 5

fig. 6

Beadweaving

STAR

1 Round 1: Thread a needle onto 24 in. of thread, pick up four 3mm bicone crystals, and form the beads into a ring by sewing through all the beads again, leaving an 8-in. tail. Step up through the first 3mm **[fig. 1]**.

2 Round 2: Pick up a 3.4mm drop bead, and sew through the next 3mm. Repeat three times, and step up through the first drop bead picked up in this step **[fig. 2]**.

3 Round 3: Pick up an 8º seed bead, and sew through the next drop bead in the previous round. Repeat three times, and step up through the first 8º picked up in this step **[fig. 3]**. Sew through the four 8ºs picked up in round 3 and the first one again, so round 3 sits on top of round 1. Step down through the next drop bead in round 2 **[fig. 4]**.

4 Round 4: Pick up a 15º seed bead, a drop bead, and a 15º, and sew through the next drop bead in round 2. Repeat three times, and retrace the thread path to secure. End the working thread **[fig. 5]**.

5 Thread a needle on the tail thread, pick up a 15º, and sew through the next 3mm in round 1. Repeat three times, and end the tail **[fig. 6]**.

Tools & Materials
For all accessories

Tools/supplies
- Fireline 6 lb. test
- Beading needles, #12
- Thread burner
- Scissors
- **2** pairs of chainnose or bentnose pliers (or one of each)
- Grooved looping pliers
- Flush cutters
- Ruler

Freestanding Wishbone Link, Attached Wishbone Link, or Wishbone Drop
- 1½ in. 20-gauge sterling silver wire
- **1–3** 3.4mm drop beads (Miyuki 260, aqua AB)

Star
- **4** 3mm bicone crystals (Swarovski 5328, turquoise)
- **8** 3.4mm drop beads (Miyuki 421D, cream ceylon)
- **4** 8º seed beads (Matsuno 421B, opaque luster cream)
- **12** 15º seed beads (Matsuno 633, aqua silver-lined rainbow)

Materials for Necklace, Bracelet, and Earrings on page 83

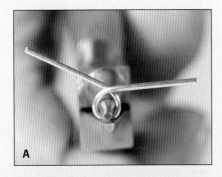

Wirework

WISHBONE LINK

Freestanding

1 Cut 1½ in. of wire. Center the wire in the second groove of the grooved looping pliers. Using your fingers, bend the wire around the round jaw, crossing the ends one over the other. As you bend, make sure that even lengths of wire remain on both ends **[A]**. Remove the wire from the pliers.

2 String a drop bead on one end of the wire. Position a wire end in the first groove of the grooved looping pliers. Turn the drop bead so the drop end faces down **[B]**. Using your left thumb and forefinger to keep the bead from sliding all the way down the wire, curl the end of the wire down and in and around the drop bead to form a closed loop around the drop bead **[C]**. Repeat on the other side **[D]**.

WISHBONE LINK

Attached

1 Cut 1½ in. of wire. Center the wire in the second groove of the grooved looping pliers. Use your fingers to bend the wire into a U shape **[E]**.

2 Place the wire through an 8º on a Star component. Center the wire so the bottom of the U sits in the 8º **[F]**. Using your fingers, hold onto both ends of the U-shaped wire and cross them over one another. As you bend, make sure that even lengths of wire remain on both ends **[G]**.

3 As in step 2 and photos B and C, string a drop bead on one end of the wire, position the end in the grooved looping pliers, and form a closed loop around the drop bead. Repeat on the other side **[H]**.

WISHBONE DROP

One-Drop

1 Follow step 1 of "Wishbone Link, Freestanding." String a drop bead onto the wire so its sits in the bottom of the U shape. Using your fingers, hold onto both ends of the U-shaped wire and cross them over one another. As you bend, make sure that even lengths of wire remain on both ends **[I]**.

2 Position a wire end in the first groove of the grooved looping pliers. Curl the end of the wire down and in to form a closed loop. Repeat on the other side **[J]**.

Three-Drop

1 Follow step 1 of "Wishbone Drop, One-Drop."

2 Follow step 2 of "Wishbone Link, Freestanding" **[K]**.

G

H

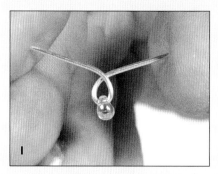

I

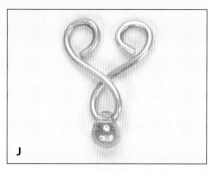

J

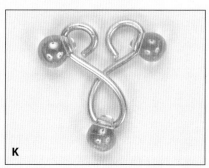

K

Materials

For each accessory

Necklace, 16 in.

- **17** Stars
- 6 ft. 20-gauge sterling silver wire to make 33 Attached Wishbone Links, 2 Freestanding Wishbone Links, and One-Drop Wishbone Drop
- **20** ⅛-in. 20-gauge bright aluminum jump rings
- **20** ³⁄₃₂-in. 20-gauge bright aluminum jump rings
- 10mm ring/22mm bar sterling silver toggle clasp

Bracelet, 7 in.

- **6** Stars
- 2 ft. 20-gauge sterling silver wire to make 12 Attached Wishbone Links
- **4** ⅛-in. 20-gauge bright aluminum jump rings
- **10** ³⁄₃₂-in. 20-gauge bright aluminum jump rings
- 10mm ring/22mm bar sterling silver toggle clasp

Earrings, 1¼ in.

- **2** Stars
- **2** ⅛-in. 20-gauge bright aluminum jump rings
- **4** ³⁄₃₂-in. 20-gauge bright aluminum jump rings
- 8 in. 20-gauge sterling silver wire to make 2 Attached Wishbone Links and 2 Three-Drop Wishbone Drops
- Pair of silver earring findings

▶**TIP** 3.4mm drops are threaded onto wire to make the decorative the links in this section. You may need to try several drops before you find one with an opening large enough for the wire to fit through because the drop shapes vary and the holes are not uniformly sized.

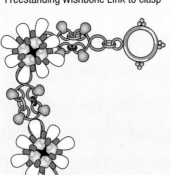

Freestanding Wishbone Link to clasp

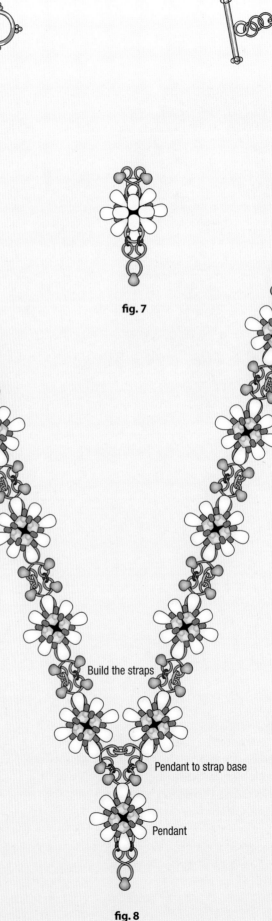

Accessories

NECKLACE

Setup

1 Make 17 Stars following steps 1–5 of "Star."

2 Attach a Wishbone Link to a Star following steps 1–3 of "Wishbone Link, Attached."

3 Attach a Wishbone Link to each of two 8⁰s opposite each other on a Star following steps 1–3 of "Wishbone Link, Attached." Repeat to make 14 components.

4 Attach a Wishbone Link to each of two 8⁰s opposite each other on a Star following steps 1–3 of "Wishbone Link, Attached," but in step 3 on one Attached Link, do not string a drop bead. Repeat to make two components, but string the drop bead on the opposite loop. These components will be attached to the pendant at assembly.

5 Make two Freestanding Wishbone Links following steps 1–2, "Wishbone Link, Freestanding."

6 Make a One-Drop Wishbone Drop following steps 1–2, "Wishbone Drop, One-Drop."

Pendant Assembly

Pick up a Star with an Attached Wishbone Link. Attach a ⅛-in. jump ring to the 8⁰ opposite the Attached Wishbone Link. Using two 3⁄32-in. jump rings, attach the One-Drop Wishbone to the ⅛-in. jump ring **[fig. 7]**.

Necklace Assembly [fig. 8]

1 To build the strap base, pick up the two Stars with a single drop on opposite loops of

fig. 7

Build the straps

Pendant to strap base

Pendant

fig. 8

Attached Wishbone Links created in Step 4 of Setup. Using two ³⁄₃₂-in. jump rings, join the Attached Wishbone Link on the pendant to the Attached Wishbone Links with single drops. Join each inner loop using a ⅛-in. jump ring.

2 To build the necklace straps, connect the Attached Wishbone Links using ⅛-in. jump rings on the outer portion of each strap and ³⁄₃₂-in. jump rings on the inner portion. Attach a Freestanding Wishbone Link to each strap end in the same manner. Use ⅛-in. jump rings to attach one half of the clasp to each end Freestanding Wishbone Link.

BRACELET

Setup

1 Make six Stars following steps 1–5 of "Star." Attach a Wishbone Link to each of two 8⁰s opposite each other on each Star following Steps 1–3 of "Wishbone Link, Attached."

Assembly

Connect the Attached Wishbone Links using ³⁄₃₂-in. jump rings. Attach an end Wishbone Link to each half of the toggle clasp using two ⅛-in. jump rings **[fig. 9]**.

EARRINGS

Setup

1 Make two Stars following steps 1–5 of "Star." Attach one Wishbone Link to each Star following Steps 1–3 of "Wishbone Link, Attached."

2 Make two Three-Drop Wishbone Drops, following steps 1 and 2 of "Wishbone Drop, Three-Drop."

Assembly

Attach a ⅛-in. jump ring to the 8⁰ opposite the Attached Wishbone Link **[fig. 10]**. Attach an earring finding to the ⅛-in. jump ring. Using two ³⁄₃₂-in. jump rings, connect a Three-Drop Wishbone to the Attached Wishbone Link **[fig. 11]**. Assemble a second earring.

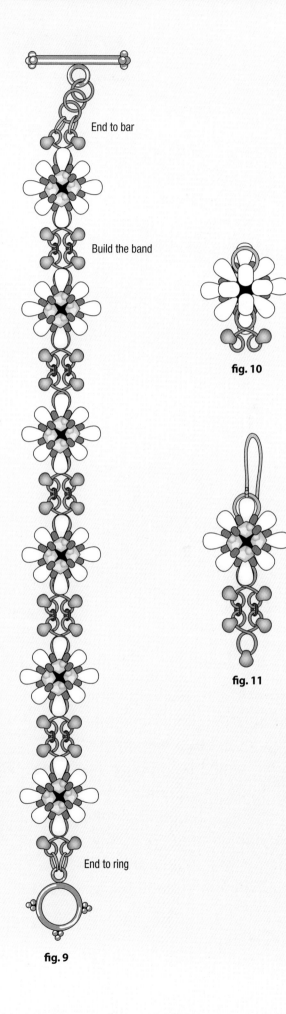

End to bar

Build the band

End to ring

fig. 9

fig. 10

fig. 11

Give It a Swirl

Play fearlessly with your beadwork and wire. Bend, wrap, twist, turn, and try different things without worry. It will open up possibilities for new design elements as well as whole new designs. Curving a Herringbone Strip led me to design the necklace pendant in this set. Lining up multiple strips gave me the necklace strap. Connect them with wire, of course. But what does that look like? More play; more time goes by before I see the connection that looks and feels right.

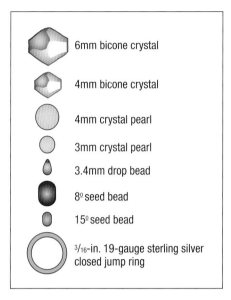

6mm bicone crystal

4mm bicone crystal

4mm crystal pearl

3mm crystal pearl

3.4mm drop bead

8º seed bead

15º seed bead

3/16-in. 19-gauge sterling silver closed jump ring

Beadweaving

HERRINGBONE STRIP

1 Round 1: Thread a needle onto the length of thread indicated in the accessory directions, pick up four 15º seed beads, and form the beads into a ring by sewing through all the beads again, leaving an 8-in. tail. Step up through the first 15º **[fig. 1]**.

2 Round 2: Pick up two 15ºs, and sew through the next 15º in the previous round. Repeat three times, and step up through the first 15º picked up in this step **[fig. 2]**.

3 Round 3: Working in herringbone stitch, pick up two 15ºs, sew down through the next 15º in round 2, and sew up through the following 15º. Repeat this stitch three times, and step up through the first 15º picked up in this step **[fig. 3]**.

4 Round 4: Pick up two 15ºs, sew down through the next 15º in round 3, pick up an 8º seed bead, and sew up through the next 15º. Repeat these two stitches three times, and step up through the first 15º picked up in this step **[fig. 4]**.

5 Round 5: Pick up a 15º, and sew down through the next three 15ºs in rounds 4, 3 and 2 to form a point at the end of round 4 **[fig. 5, a–b]**. Pick up a 15º (which starts the raised portion of the component and sits at an angle between each 15º in round 2), and sew up through the next three 15ºs in rounds 2, 3, and 4 **[fig. 5, b–c]**. Pick up two 15ºs, and sew down through the next three 15ºs in rounds 4, 3, and 2. Pick up a 15º, and sew up through the next three 15ºs in rounds 2, 3, and 4 **[fig. 5, c–d]**. Repeat the thread path **[fig. 5, d–e]**. Pick up a 15º, and sew up through the next three 15ºs in rounds 2, 3, and 4. Pick up two 15ºs, and sew down through the next three 15ºs in rounds 4, 3, and 2. Pick up a 15º, and sew up through the next 15º in round 2 and down through the following 15º in the same round. Step up through the first raised 15º picked up in this step **[fig. 5, e–f]**.

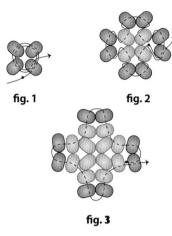

fig. 1

fig. 2

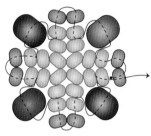

fig. 3

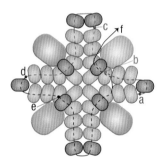

fig. 4

fig. 5

Tools & Materials

For all accessories

Tools/supplies

- Fireline 6 lb. test
- Beading needles, #12
- Thread burner
- Scissors
- **2** pairs of chainnose pliers, including one large pair, or chainnose and bentnose pliers
- Grooved looping pliers
- Flush cutters
- Ruler

Herringbone Strip

- 4mm bicone crystals (Preciosa 451 69 302, aqua bohemica)
- 8º seed beads (Miyuki 462, metallic gold iris)
- 15º seed beads (Toho 999, gold-lined rainbow black diamond)

Note: The length of the Herringbone Strip varies by the accessory. Refer to the specific accessory for bead quantities.

Materials for Necklace, Bracelet, and Ring on page 89

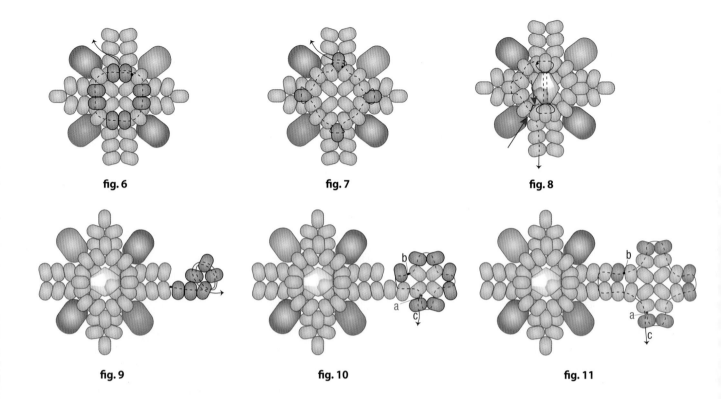

fig. 6

fig. 7

fig. 8

fig. 9

fig. 10

fig. 11

6 Pick up two 15ºs, and sew through the next raised 15º added in the previous step. Repeat three times, and step up through the first 15º picked up in this step [**fig. 6**].

7 Pick up a 15º, and sew through the next three raised 15ºs. Repeat three times, and step up through the first 15º picked up in this step [**fig. 7**].

8 Pick up a 4mm bicone crystal, and sew through the 15º opposite the one the thread is exiting. Sew back through the 4mm and the 15º your thread exited at the start of this step. Sew through the next six raised 15ºs. To exit, sew through to the closest 15º on the beadwork base. (This 15º is hard to see because it is under a raised 15º.) Sew through the next three 15ºs on the beadwork base, and exit [**fig. 8**].

▶ **TIP** In figures 8 and 14, red arrows point to the hidden 15º in the base layer.

9 Pick up six 15ºs, skip the first two 15ºs just picked up, and sew back through the last four 15ºs to form a loop. Check that the loop is tight against the two skipped beads, and sew through the first 15º in the loop again [**fig. 9**].

10 Pick up two 15ºs, and sew through the next 15º in the loop. Repeat twice [**fig. 10, a–b**]. Pick up a 15º, sew up through the second skipped 15º in the loop created in step 9, and sew through the next two 15ºs as shown [**fig. 10, b–c**].

11 Pick up two 15ºs, sew down through the next 15º in the previous round, and sew up through the following 15º. Repeat twice [**fig. 11, a–b**]. Pick up a 15º, and close the gap in the base by sewing through the 15º at the end of the previous section. Sew through the beadwork as shown [**fig. 11, b–c**].

12 Pick up two 15ºs, sew down through the next 15º in the previous round, pick up an 8º, and sew up through the next 15º in the previous round. Repeat these

two stitches twice [**fig. 12, a–b**]. Without picking up any beads, sew down through the next 15º in the previous round, pick up an 8º, and sew up through the next 15º in the previous round. Step up through the first 15º picked up in this step [**fig. 12, b–c**].

13 To form a point at the end of round 4, pick up a 15º, and sew down through the next three 15ºs in rounds 4, 3, and 2 [**fig. 13, a–b**]. To start the raised portion of the section, pick up a 15º, and sew up through the next three 15ºs in rounds 2, 3, and 4 [**fig. 13, b–c**]. Pick up two 15ºs, and sew down through the next three 15ºs in rounds 4, 3, and 2. Repeat path b–c [**fig. 13, c–d**], and then repeat path a–b. Pick up a 15º, and sew up through the next 15º in round 2 and down through the next 15º in round 2. Pick up a 15º, and sew up through the next 15º in round 2 and down through the next the 15º in round 2. Step up through the first raised 15º picked up in this step [**fig. 13, d–e**].

14 Repeat steps 6 and 7.

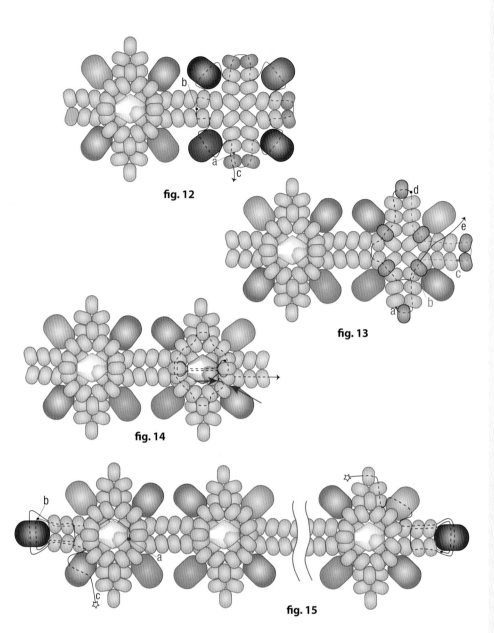

fig. 12

fig. 13

fig. 14

fig. 15

15 Pick up a 4mm crystal, sew through the 15º opposite the one the thread is exiting, and sew back through the 4mm and the 15º exited at the start of this step. Sew through the raised 15ºs as shown. To exit, sew through to the closest 15º on the beadwork base. (This 15º is hard to see because it is under a raised 15º.) Sew through the next three 15ºs on the beadwork base, and exit **[fig. 14]**.

16 Repeat steps 9–15 to make additional sections as needed.

17 Pick up an 8º. Sew through the beadwork as shown **[fig. 15, right side]**, and end the working thread. Thread a needle on the tail, and sew through the path as shown **[fig. 15, a–b]**. Pick up an 8º, and sew through the beadwork as shown **[fig. 15, b–c]**. End the tail.

Materials
For each accessory

Necklace, 17 in.
- **10** three-section Herringbone Strips
- Nine-section Herringbone Strip
- **39** 4mm bicone crystals (Preciosa 451 69 302, aqua bohemica)
- **11** 3.4mm drop beads (Miyuki 260, aqua AB)
- **48** 3mm pearls (Swarovski 5810, gold)
- **232** 8º seed beads (Miyuki 462, metallic gold iris)
- 5 grams 15º seed beads (Toho 999, gold-lined rainbow black diamond)
- 3 ft. 20-gauge titanium craft wire to make 11 Swirls
- **2** 3/16-in. 19-gauge sterling silver closed jump rings
- 14x5mm sterling silver lobster claw clasp

Bracelet, 7¼ in.
- 14-section Herringbone Strip
- **14** 4mm bicone crystals (Preciosa 451 69 302, aqua bohemica)
- **2** 3.4mm drop beads (Miyuki 260, aqua AB)
- **26** 3mm pearls (Swarovski 5810, gold)
- **68** 8º seed beads (Miyuki 462, metallic gold iris)
- 2 grams 15º seed beads (Toho 999, gold-lined rainbow black diamond)
- 6 in. 20-gauge titanium craft wire to make 2 Swirls
- **2** 3/16-in. 19-gauge sterling silver closed jump rings
- 14x5mm sterling silver lobster claw clasp

Ring
- Three-section Herringbone Strip
- 6mm bicone crystal (Preciosa 451 69 302, aqua bohemica)
- **2** 4mm bicone crystals (Preciosa 451 69 302, aqua bohemica)
- **4** 4mm pearls (Swarovski 5810, gold)
- **12** 8º seed beads (Miyuki 462, metallic gold iris)
- Gram 15º seed beads (Toho 999, gold-lined rainbow black diamond)

Wirework

▶**TIP** I use large chainnose pliers to hold the Swirl steady because the wider jaw provides extra stability.

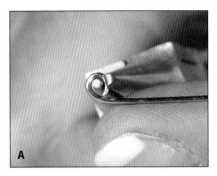

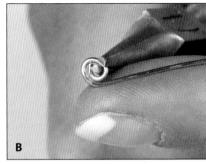

SWIRL

1 Cut 2½ in. of wire. Place one end of the wire in the first groove of the grooved looping pliers. Roll your right hand toward you while bracing the other end of the wire with your left forefinger to create a small loop **[A]**. Reposition the pliers slightly back and continue to roll forward, starting a second loop around the first **[B]**.

2 Holding the loop with the chainnose pliers, guide the wire with your finger. Turning and keeping the wire close to the previous loop, form a second loop **[C]**.

3 Increasing the distance from the second loop, continue to guide the wire around until the third loop is about three quarters of the way around the second **[D]**.

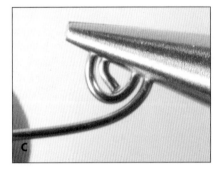

Accessories

NECKLACE

Setup

1 On 36 in. of thread, make 10 Herringbone Strips with three sections per strip following steps 1–17 of "Herringbone Strip."

2 On 60 in. of thread, make one Herringbone Strip with nine sections following steps 1–17 of "Herringbone Strip."

3 Make 10 Swirls following steps 1–3 of "Swirl."

4 Make one Swirl using 2¾ in. rather than 2½ in. of wire following steps 1–3 of "Swirl."

Strap Link

Add 24 in. of thread to a three-section Herringbone Strip, and exit next to an end 8º. Sew through the next 15º on the strip, pick up two 15ºs, and sew through the next 8º. Continue up through the next 15º in round 3 of the section and down through the next 15º in round 3, and sew through the next 8º. Repeat the pattern around the Herringbone Strip, picking up two 15ºs or a 3mm pearl as shown, and end both threads **[fig. 16]**. Repeat for the other nine strips.

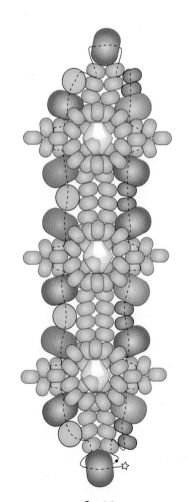

fig. 16

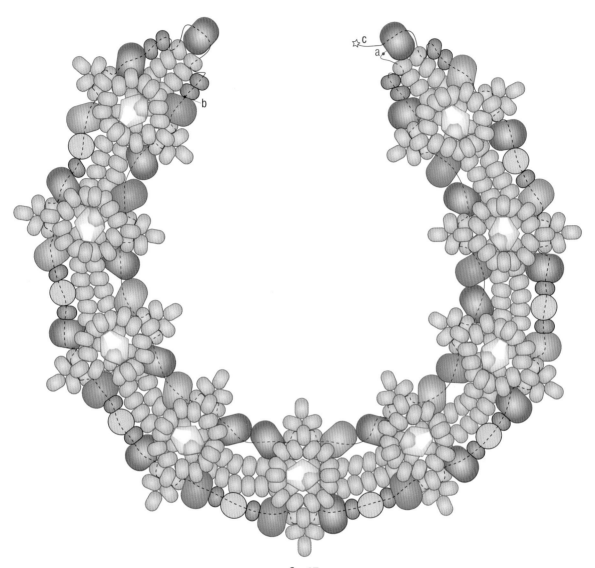

fig. 17

Pendant

Add 30 in. of thread to the nine-section Herringbone Strip, and exit next to the end 8° on the right side. Sew through the next 15° on the strip, pick up two 15°s, and sew through the next 8°. Without picking up any beads, sew through the next nine sections of the Herringbone Strip [**fig. 17, a–b**]. Pick up two 15°s, sew through the 15° and the 8° on the end of the strip, and sew down through the next 15°. Pick up two 15°s, and sew through the next 8°. Continue around the outer portion of the pendant, picking up 3mm pearls or 15°s and following the pattern as shown, and end both threads [**fig. 17, b–c**].

TIP Closed jump rings are shown in bright green.

fig. 18

E

F

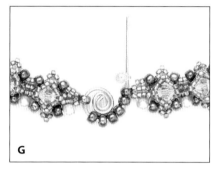

G

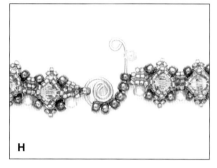

H

I

Right Side Strap Assembly [fig. 18]

1 Lay a Strap Link flat **[E]**.

2 Starting with the unembellished inner edge of the Strap Link, thread the straight end of the Swirl through the upper end 8º on the Strap Link. Thread five 8ºs onto the wire **[F]**. Starting with the pearl edge, thread the wire through the lower end 8º on a second Strap Link. Thread a 3.4mm drop bead on the wire **[G]**.

3 Holding the end of the Strap Link and the Swirl steady, place the end of the wire in the first groove of the grooved looping pliers and make a loop **[H]**. Grip the loop with large chainnose pliers and curve the wire inward until it sits on top of the larger swirl **[I]**.

4 Repeat steps 2 and 3 to attach the next Swirl to the upper end 8º in the second Strap Link and to a third Strap Link. Connect five Strap Links in this manner to build one side of the strap. Thread the

straight end of a Swirl through the end 8º on the last Strap Link. Thread five 8ºs, a ³⁄₁₆-in. closed jump ring, and a 3.4mm drop bead onto the wire **[J]**. Repeat step 3 to complete the attachment.

5 Attach a lobster claw clasp to the ³⁄₁₆-in. closed jump ring.

Left Side Strap Assembly [fig. 18]

1 Lay a Strap Link flat **[K]**.

2 Repeat steps 2–4 of "Right Side Strap," keeping in mind the direction of the left strap is reversed.

Attaching the Pendant [fig. 18]

Starting from the Right Side Strap, thread the 2¾-in. Swirl through the end 8º in the Strap and the end 8º in the right side of the Pendant. Thread four 8ºs on the wire. Continue to thread the wire through the end 8º in the left side of the Pendant and the end 8º in the Left Side Strap. Thread a 3.4mm drop bead on the wire **[L]**. Repeat step 3 of "Right Side Strap Assembly."

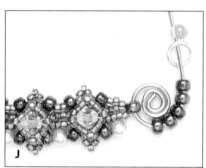

J

K

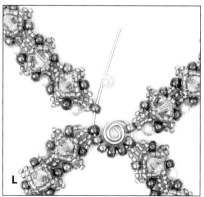

L

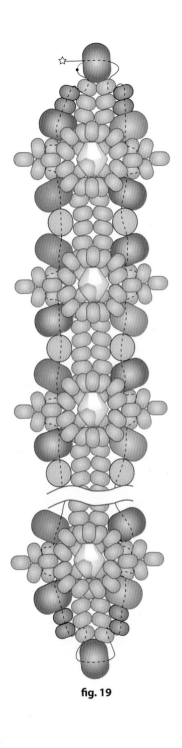

fig. 19

fig. 20

BRACELET

Setup

1 On 60 in. of thread, make one Herringbone Strip 14 sections long following steps 1–17 of "Herringbone Strip."

2 Add 24 in. of thread to the 14-section Herringbone Strip, exit next to an end 8º, and sew through the next 15º in the strip. Pick up two 15ºs, and sew through the next 8º. Sew up through the next 15º in round 3 of the section and down through the next 15º in the same round. Sew through the next 8º, pick up a 3mm pearl, and sew down the outside edge of the herringbone strip, adding a 3mm pearl between sets of 8ºs. After exiting the last 8º, pick up two 15ºs and sew up through the last 15º and the end 8º. Repeat the pattern on the other side. End both threads [**fig. 19**].

3 Make two Swirls following Steps 1–3 of "Swirl."

Assembly

1 Thread the straight end of a Swirl through either end 8º on the 14-section Herringbone strip. Thread five 8ºs, a ³⁄₁₆-in. closed jump ring, and a 3.4mm drop bead on the wire.

2 To complete the attachment of the Swirl to the bracelet band, follow step 3 of "Right Side Strap."

3 Repeat steps 1 and 2 on the opposite end of the bracelet band, reversing the direction from which you thread the wire through the end 8º. Attach a lobster claw clasp to the closed jump ring on one Swirl [**fig. 20**].

RING

1 On 36 in. of thread, make one Herringbone Strip three sections long following steps 1–16 of "Herringbone Strip" with the following alterations: The ring has one less two-bead set between each section. To accommodate the shorter length, in step 9, pick up five 15ºs instead of six. Skip the first 15º just added, and sew back through the last four 15ºs to form a loop. In step 10, after completing a–b, pick up a 15º, and close the gap in the base by sewing through the 15º at the end of the previous section. In step 11 [**fig. 11, b–c**], there is not an additional bead to pick up, as the gap is already closed. Continue with the remaining steps, keeping in mind when following the thread path the lack of a two-bead set between the first and second and the second and third sections. When completing the second section in step 8, pick up a 6mm bicone crystal instead of a 4mm.

2 After completing the three-section Herringbone Strip, and using the same thread, sew up through the end 15º next to the 15º the thread is exiting. Pick up a 15º, and sew through the next 8º. Pick up a 15º, and sew up through the 15º in round 4 of the first section and through the next 15º. This is the 15º that forms the point. Pick up a 4mm pearl, and sew through the 15º that forms the point in section two. Pick up a 4mm pearl and sew through the 15º that forms the point in the third section and down through the next 15º. Pick up a 15º, sew through the next 8º, pick up a 15º, and sew up through the last 15º on the strip [**fig. 21**]. Repeat on the other side of the strip.

3 To make the band, pick up two 15ºs, and sew down through the next two 15ºs opposite the 15º the thread is exiting. Sew up through the opposite two 15ºs, and sew through the first 15º picked up [**fig. 22**]. Continue to add two-bead sets in this manner until the band is long enough to fit comfortably around the desired finger. Sew through the sets of 15ºs on the opposite end to join and complete the band. End the threads.

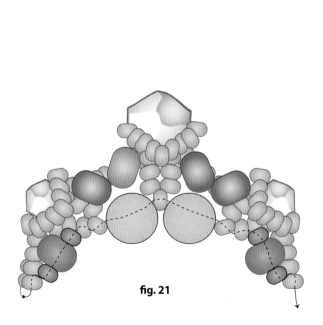

fig. 21

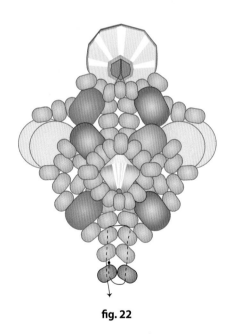

fig. 22

Cosmic Chorus

To me, the words "cosmic chorus" suggest "the science of everything" linked with "the repeated part of a song." This design links my "everything," beads, with repeated wire components. You now have the materials, the tools, and the expertise to create your own vibrant rendition.

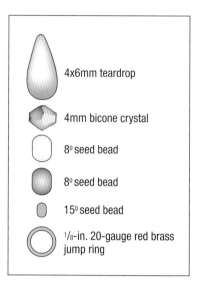

4x6mm teardrop

4mm bicone crystal

8º seed bead

8º seed bead

15º seed bead

⅛-in. 20-gauge red brass jump ring

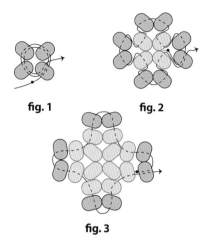

fig. 1

fig. 2

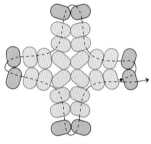

fig. 3

fig. 4

fig. 5

Beadweaving

CRYSTAL STAR

1 Round 1: Thread a needle onto 30 in. of thread, pick up four 15ºs seed beads, and form the beads into a ring by sewing through all four beads again, leaving a 6-in. tail. Step up through the first 15º [**fig. 1**].

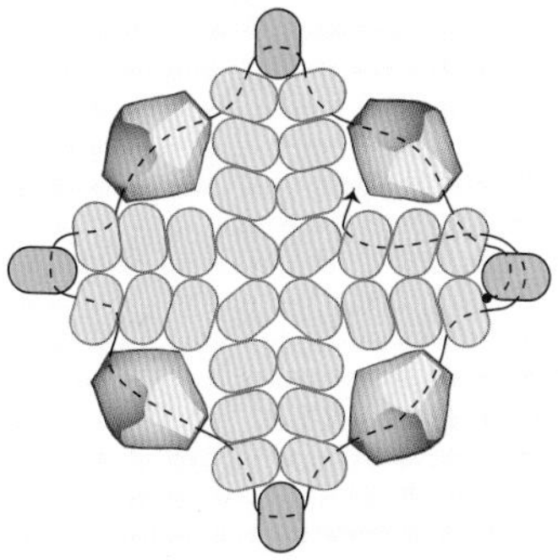

2 Round 2: Pick up two 15ºs, and sew through the next 15º in the previous row. Repeat three times, and step up through the first 15º picked up in this step [**fig. 2**].

3 Round 3: Pick up two 15ºs, sew down through the next 15º in round 2, and sew up through the next 15º. Repeat three times, and step up through the first 15º picked up in this step [**fig. 3**].

4 Round 4: Pick up two 15ºs, sew down through the next two 15ºs in rounds 3 and 2, and sew up through the next two 15ºs in rounds 2 and 3. Repeat three times, and step up through the first 15º picked up in this step [**fig. 4**].

5 Round 5: Pick up a 15º, and sew down through the next 15º in round 4. Pick up a 4mm bicone crystal, and sew up through the next 15º in round 4. Repeat three times, and step up through the first 15º picked up in this step. Sew down through the next three 15ºs in rounds 4, 3, and 2 as shown [**fig. 5**].

Tools & Materials
For all accessories

Tools/supplies
- Fireline 6 lb. test
- Beading needles, #12
- Thread burner
- Scissors
- **2** pairs of chainnose or bentnose pliers (or one of each)
- Grooved looping pliers
- Flush cutters
- Ruler

Crystal Star Link
- **6** 4mm bicone crystals (Preciosa 451 69 302, capri gold)
- **12** 8º seed beads (Matsuno 333, Ceylon peachy pink)
- **92** 15º seed beads (Miyuki 365, transparent light shell pink luster)
- **4** ⅛-in. 20-gauge red brass jump rings

Teardrop Moon Link
- **16** 4x6mm teardrop beads (Czech glass, light topaz)
- **4** 8º seed beads (Matsuno F634, silver-lined rainbow matte)
- **4** ⅛-in. 20-gauge red brass jump rings

Materials for Necklace, Bracelet, and Earrings on page 99

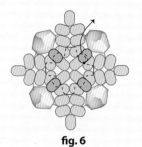

fig. 6

fig. 7

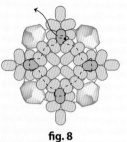

fig. 8

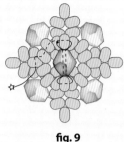

fig. 9

6 Pick up a 15º. This 15º starts the raised portion of the Crystal Star and sits at an angle between each 15º in round 2. Sew up through the next 15º in round 2 and down through the adjacent 15º in round 2. Repeat three more times, and step up through the first raised 15º picked up in this step [**fig. 6**].

7 Pick up two 15ºs, and sew through the next raised 15º. Repeat three times, and step up through the first 15º picked up in this step [**fig. 7**].

8 Pick up a 15º, and sew through the next three raised 15ºs. Repeat three times, and step up through the first 15º picked up in this step [**fig. 8**].

9 Pick up a 4mm, and sew through the 15º opposite the 15º the thread is exiting. Sew back through the 4mm and the 15º exited at the start. End both the working and tail threads [**fig. 9**].

10 Work as in steps 1–4 to make another Crystal Star. End the tail thread.

11 Position the piece in progress against the back of the Crystal Star completed in step 10, aligning the working thread with the direction of the holes of the crystal. Join the two pieces by sewing through the 15º that forms the point on the completed piece, and sew down through the next 15º in round 4 of the piece in progress. Sew through the next 4mm on the completed piece, and sew up through the next 15º in round 4 of the piece in progress. Repeat three times, step up through the 15º that forms the point, and continue down

fig. 10

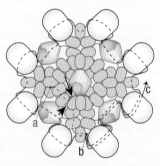

fig. 11

through the next three 15ºs in rounds 4, 3, and 2 on the piece in progress [**fig. 10**].

12 Make the raised portion following steps 6–9, but do not end the working thread at the end of step 9.

13 Sew through the next two raised 15ºs, and sew through the beadwork to exit the closest 15º on the beadwork base. (This 15º is hard to see because it is under a raised 15º. Two arrows point it out in **fig. 11**.) Sew through the next two 15ºs on the beadwork base, and exit the 15º that forms a point [**fig. 11, a–b**]. Pick up an 8º seed bead, sew through the next 4mm, pick up an 8º, and step up through the next 15º that forms a point. Repeat three times. Sew back though the first 8º picked up in this step, the next 4mm, and the following 8º [**fig. 11, b–c**].

14 Pick up an 8º, and sew though the next 8º, 4mm, and 8º. Repeat three times, and sew back though the first 8º picked up in this step. End the thread [**fig. 12**].

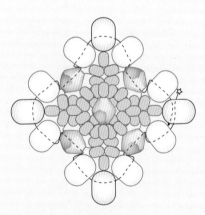

fig. 12

TEARDROP MOON

1 Round 1: Thread a needle onto 24 in. of thread, pick up four 4x6mm teardrop beads, and form the beads into a ring by sewing through all four beads again, leaving a 6-in. tail. Step up through the first bead [**fig. 13**].

2 Round 2: Pick up a teardrop, and sew through the next teardrop. Repeat three more times, and step up through the first teardrop picked up in this step [**fig. 14**].

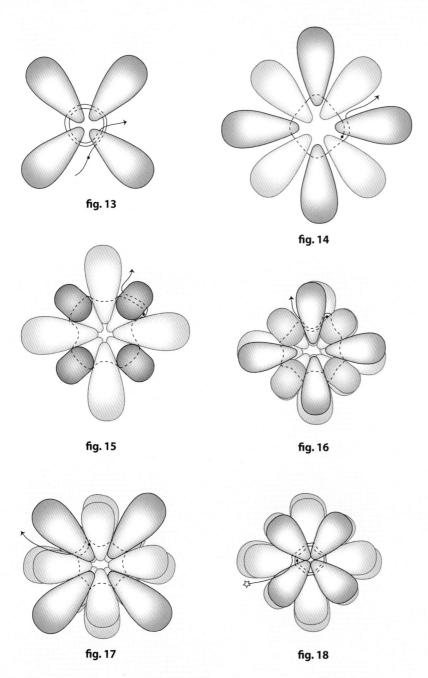

fig. 13

fig. 14

fig. 15

fig. 16

fig. 17

fig. 18

Materials
For each accessory

Necklace, 28 in.
- **4** Crystal Star Links
- **3** Teardrop Moon Links
- **6** 8º seed beads (Matsuno 333, Ceylon peachy pink)
- **11 ft.** 20-gauge red brass wire to make 25 Six-Loop Links and Toggle Clasp
- **185** ⅛-in. 20-gauge red brass jump rings (includes quantity needed to make 4 Crystal Star Links and 3 Teardrop Moon Links)

Bracelet, 7 in.
- **3** Crystal Star Links
- **6** 8º seed beads (Matsuno 333, Ceylon peachy pink)
- **3 ft.** 20-gauge red brass wire to make 4 Six-Loop Links and Toggle Clasp
- **46** ⅛-in. 20-gauge red brass jump rings (includes quantity needed to make 3 Crystal Star Links)

Earrings, 2 in.
- **2** Crystal Star Links
- **10 in.** 20-gauge red brass wire to make 2 Six-Loop Links
- **20** ⅛-in. 20-gauge red brass jump rings (includes quantity needed to make 2 Crystal Star Links)
- **Pair** of gold-filled earring findings

3 Round 3: Pick up an 8º seed bead, and sew through the next teardrop. Repeat three more times, and step up through the first 8º picked up in this step [**fig. 15**].

4 Round 4: Pick up a teardrop, and sew through the next 8º. Repeat three more times, and step up through the first teardrop picked up in this step [**fig. 16**].

5 Round 5: Pick up a teardrop, and sew through the next teardrop in the previous round. Repeat three more times, and step up through the first teardrop picked up in this step [**fig. 17**]. To pull the teardrops tightly together, sew through all four teardrops picked up in round 5 again, reinforce the thread path to secure, and end the threads [**fig. 18**].

fig. 19

Wirework

CRYSTAL STAR LINK

Attach a jump ring to four 8°s on a Crystal Star as shown [**fig. 19**].

TEARDROP MOON LINK

Attach a jump ring to each of the four 8°s on a Teardrop Moon.

SIX-LOOP LINK

1 Cut 4 in. wire. Working in the third groove of the grooved looping pliers, create a P-shaped loop following "Making a P-shaped loop with grooved looping pliers" (p. 20).

2 With the P-shaped loop facing up, place the wire in the third groove, leaving about ¹⁄₁₆ in. from the outermost curve

of the previous loop [**A**]. Wrap the wire around the roundnose jaw. Reposition the pliers slightly forward and wrap the wire until it crosses at the bottom center of the loop [**B**]. Repeat to make the next three loops. Flush-cut the wire end so you have approximately ½ in. of straight wire extending from the outermost curve of the fifth loop. With the loops facing up, position the end of the wire in the third groove and repeat step 1 to make the sixth loop [**C**].

TOGGLE CLASP

1 To make the toggle loop, cut 2¾ in. of wire. Using a Sharpie as a mandrel, find the midpoint of the wire and cross one wire end over the other to form a loop [**D**].

2 Twist one end of the wire over the other to close the loop [**E**], leaving approximately ½ in. of straight wire on each end. If you have extra wire, flush-cut it to ½ in.

3 String an 8° onto one end of the wire so it butts up against the end of the loop. Place the end of the wire in the first groove of the grooved looping pliers, leaving approximately ¹⁄₁₆ in. extending from the end of the jaw [**F**]. Roll the pliers toward the loop until the wire end is flush against the loop [**G**]. Use chainnose or roundnose pliers to adjust as needed. Repeat on the other side.

4 To make the toggle bar, cut 1⅝ in. of wire. Center the wire in the second groove. Using your fingers, cross the wire ends over one another, making sure that even lengths of wire remain on both ends [**H**].

5 String two 8°s onto one wire end so they butt up against the end of the loop. Place the end of the wire in the first groove, and curl the end of the wire up and in to form a closed loop [**I**]. Repeat on the other side.

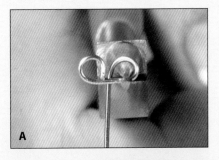
A

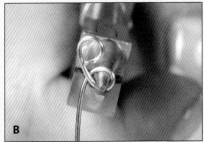
B

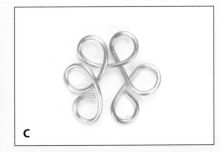
C

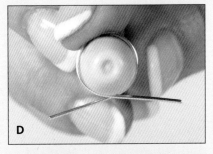
D

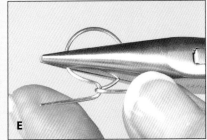
E

F

G

H

I

Strand assembly

Clasp to strand ends

Clasp to band

Accessories

NECKLACE
Setup
1 Make four Crystal Stars following steps 1–14 of "Crystal Star," and make four Crystal Star Links following "Crystal Star Link."

2 Make three Teardrop Moons following steps 1–5 of "Teardrop Moon," and make three Teardrop Moon Links following "Teardrop Moon Link."

3 Make 25 Six-Loop Links followings steps 1 and 2 of "Six-Loop Link."

4 Make a Toggle Clasp following steps 1–5 of "Toggle Clasp."

Assembly
Use jump rings to join the Six-Loop Links, the Crystal Star Links, and the Teardrop Moon Links following the pattern as shown [**fig. 20**]. Use jump rings to attach half of the clasp to each strand end.

BRACELET
Setup
1 Make three Crystal Stars following steps 1–14 of "Crystal Star," and make three Crystal Star Links following "Crystal Star Link."

2 Make four Six-Loop Links following steps 1 and 2 of "Six-Loop Link."

3 Make a Toggle Clasp following steps 1–5 of "Toggle Clasp."

Assembly
Use jump rings to join Six-Loop Links and Crystal Star Links as shown [**fig. 21**]. Use jump rings to attach half of the clasp to each end.

EARRINGS
Setup
1 Make two Crystal Stars following steps 1–14 of "Crystal Star."

2 Make two Six-Loop Links following steps 1 and 2 of "Six-Loop Link."

Assembly
Attach a jump ring to two 8°s on a Crystal Star as shown. Use five jump rings to attach the Six-Loop Link to the Crystal Star. Use three jump rings to attach the upper portion of the Six-Loop Link to an earring finding [**fig. 22**]. Assemble a second earring.

Band assembly

fig. 21

fig. 22

fig. 20

A Piece of the Past

Do you recall the stitched Triangle in Growing Frida's Flower bracelet? If not, take a peek back. The Triangle in this set has fewer stitched rounds and uses two colors of seed beads instead of just one. This stitched component can stand on its own, but it is glorious when coupled with crystals, wire, and chain.

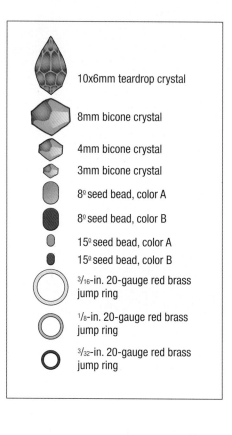

10x6mm teardrop crystal

8mm bicone crystal

4mm bicone crystal

3mm bicone crystal

8º seed bead, color A

8º seed bead, color B

15º seed bead, color A

15º seed bead, color B

³/₁₆-in. 20-gauge red brass jump ring

¹/₈-in. 20-gauge red brass jump ring

³/₃₂-in. 20-gauge red brass jump ring

Beadweaving

TRIANGLE

1 Round 1: Thread a needle onto 36 in. of thread, pick up four color-A 15º seed beads, and form the beads into a ring by sewing through the first A 15º, leaving an 8-in. tail [**fig. 1**].

2 Round 2: Pick up two A 15ºs, and sew through the next A 15º in the previous round. Repeat three times, and step up through the first A 15º picked up in this step [**fig. 2**].

3 Round 3: Pick up two A 15ºs, sew down through the next A 15º in the previous round, and sew up through the next A 15º. Repeat three times, and step up through the first A 15º picked up in this step [**fig. 3**].

4 Round 4: Pick up two A 15ºs, and sew through the next A 15º. Pick up a color-B 8º seed bead, and sew up through the next A 15º in the previous round. Repeat three times, and step up through the first A 15º picked up in this step [**fig. 4**].

5 Round 5: Pick up two A 15ºs, and sew through the next A 15º. Pick up a color-B 15º seed bead, and sew through the next B 8º. Pick up a B 15º, and sew up through the next A 15º in the previous round. Repeat three times, and step up through the first A 15º picked up in this step [**fig. 5**].

fig. 1

fig. 2

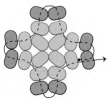

fig. 3

fig. 4

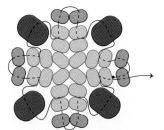

fig. 5

Tools & Materials
For all accessories

Tools/supplies
- Fireline 6 lb. test
- Beading needles, #12
- Thread burner
- Scissors
- **2** pairs of chainnose or bentnose pliers (or one of each)
- Grooved looping pliers
- Looping pliers
- Flush cutters
- Ruler

Triangle
- **3** 8º seed beads, color A (Miyuki 301, amethyst rose gold luster)
- **12** 8º seed beads, color B (Toho 502, raspberry bronze metallic)
- **60** 15º seed beads, color A (Toho 203, amethyst rose gold luster)
- **44** 15º seed beads, color B (Toho 502, raspberry bronze metallic)

Four-Loop Drop
- 4mm bicone crystal (Preciosa 451 51 681, capri gold)
- **2** 3mm bicone crystals (Preciosa 451 51 681, capri gold)
- 2½–2⅝ in. 20-gauge red brass wire

Five-Loop Drop
- 10x6mm teardrop crystal (Preciosa 451 51 681, capri gold)
- 2⅞ in. 20-gauge red brass wire

Materials for Necklace, Bracelet, and Earrings on page 106

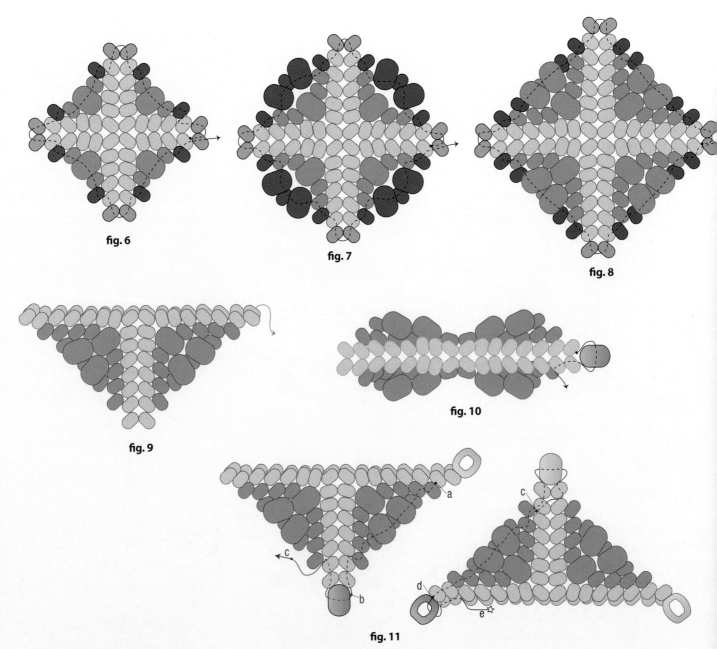

fig. 6

fig. 7

fig. 8

fig. 9

fig. 10

fig. 11

6 Round 6: Pick up two A 15ºs, and sew down through the next A 15º. Pick up a B 15º, and sew through the next B 15º, B 8º, and B 15º. Pick up a B 15º, and sew up through the next A 15º. Repeat three times, and step up through the first A 15º picked up in this step [**fig. 6**].

7 Round 7: Pick up two A 15ºs, and sew through the next A 15º. Pick up a B 15º, and sew through the next B 15º. Pick up a B 8º, B 15º, and a B 8º, and sew through the next B 15º. Pick up a B 15º, and sew up through the next A 15º. Repeat three times, and step up through the first A 15º picked up in this step [**fig. 7**]. The Triangle may start to bow and curve.

8 Round 8: Pick up two A 15ºs, and sew down through the next A 15º. Pick up a B 15º, and sew through the next B 15º. Pick up a B 15º, and sew through the next B 8º, B 15º, and B 8º. Pick up a B 15º, and sew through the next B 15º. Pick up a B 15º, and sew up through the next A 15º. Repeat three times, and step up through the first A 15º picked up in this step [**fig. 8**].

9 Fold the beadwork in half to form a Triangle [**fig. 9**]. With the fold facing you, pick up a color-A 8º seed bead, and sew through the next two A 15ºs as shown [**fig. 10**].

10 Sew though the beadwork as shown to exit an A 15º in the opposite corner [**fig. 11, a–b**]. Pick up an A 8º, and sew up through the next two A 15ºs [**fig. 11, b–c**]. Turn the Triangle over, and sew down through the A 15º that corresponds to the 15º the thread is exiting. Sew across and down through the A 15º in the corner to the right of the A 8º picked up in b–c. Sew through the A 8º and the beadwork to exit an A 15º in the opposite corner [**fig. 11, c–d**]. Pick up an A 8º, sew through the next two A 15ºs as shown, and end the threads as directed [**fig. 11, d–e**].

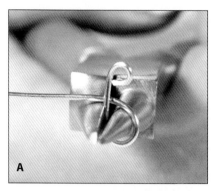

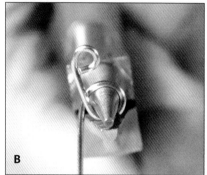

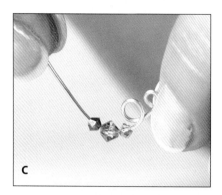

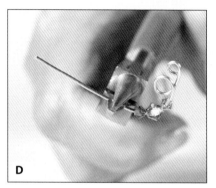

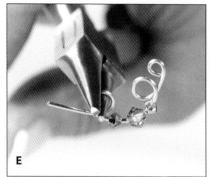

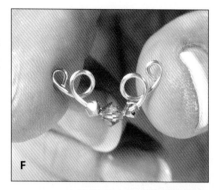

Wirework

FOUR-LOOP DROP

1 Cut 2½ in. of wire. Working in the first groove of the grooved looping pliers, create a P-shaped loop following "Making a P-shaped loop with grooved looping pliers" (p. 20).

2 With the loop facing up, place the wire in the third groove about ⅛ in. from the previous loop. Wrap the wire around the roundnose jaw until the wire tail crosses between the two loops at a 90-degree angle **[A]**. Reposition the pliers slightly forward and wrap the wire until it crosses the bottom center of the loop and the wire tail is horizontal **[B]**.

3 String a 3mm bicone crystal, a 4mm bicone crystal, and a 3mm bicone crystal onto the wire. With the thumb and forefinger of each hand, bend each end slightly up and in, creating a shallow drop in the center **[C]**.

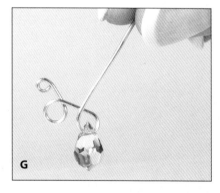

4 With the two loops facing up, place the wire in the third groove about ⅛ in. from the last 3mm crystal **[D]**. Wrap the wire around the roundnose jaw until it crosses between the last 3mm crystal and the loop at a 90-degree angle. Reposition the pliers slightly forward, and wrap the wire until it crosses the bottom center of the loop and the wire tail is horizontal **[E]**.

5 With the loops facing up, position the wire end in the first groove, and create the fourth loop in the same manner as the first.

6 With the thumb and forefinger of each hand, bend each wire end slightly up and in to adjust the curvature of the drop **[F]**.

FIVE-LOOP DROP

1 Cut 2⅞ in. of wire. Make two loops following steps 1 and 2 of "Four-Loop Drop."

2 With the two loops facing up, place the wire in the third groove of the grooved looping pliers about ⅛ in. from the previous loop. Wrap the wire loosely around the roundnose jaw until it crosses the bottom center of the loop. Pull the tail of the loop slightly out, string a 6x10mm teardrop on the loop **[G]**, and press the loop back into position. With the three loops facing up, repeat steps 2 and 5 of "Four-Loop Drop" **[H]**.

Materials

For each accessory

Necklace, 16 in.

- **22** Triangles
- **22** 8mm bicone crystals (Preciosa 451 51 681, capri gold)
- **3 ft.** 20-gauge red brass wire to make 11 Four-Loop Drops
- **7 ft.** 24-gauge red brass wire to make 22 Crystal Connectors
- **17 in.** 2mm textured 14k gold oval chain
- **50** ⅛-in. 20-gauge red brass jump rings
- **32** ³⁄₁₆-in. 20-gauge red brass jump rings
- **20x15mm** vermeil 2-strand filigree box clasp

Bracelet, 7¼ in.

- **28** Triangles
- **14** 8mm bicone crystals (Preciosa 451 51 681, capri gold)
- **10 in.** 20-gauge red brass wire to make 4 Four-Loop Drops
- **4** ³⁄₃₂-in. 20-gauge red brass jump rings
- **21** ⅛-in. 20-gauge red brass jump rings
- **8** ³⁄₁₆-in. 20-gauge red brass jump rings
- **8.5mm** gold-filled 3-strand filigree box clasp

Earrings, 2 in.

- **2** Triangles
- **13 in.** 20-gauge red brass wire to make 2 Four-Loop Drops and 2 Five-Loop Drops
- **6** ⅛-in. 20-gauge red brass jump rings
- **4** ³⁄₁₆-in. 20-gauge red brass jump rings
- Pair of gold-filled earring findings

Accessories

NECKLACE

Setup

1 Make 22 Triangles following steps 1–10 of "Triangle." End both threads in Step 10.

2 Make 11 Four-Loop Drops following steps 1–6 of "Four-Loop Drop."

3 Make 22 Crystal Connectors following "Making a wrapped loop with looping pliers" (p. 21) using 3-in. lengths of 24-gauge red brass wire and 8mm bicone crystals.

4 Cut two seven-Link (⁹⁄₁₆ in.), two 12-link (1 in.) and 10 14-link (1⅛ in.) pieces of chain.

Necklace Links

1 Use ⅛-in. jump rings for the Necklace Links and assembly unless another size is specified. Create a Necklace Link using a jump ring to join pairs of Triangles as shown [**fig. 12**]. Make a total of 11 Necklace Links.

2 Starting from the center Necklace Link, thread a jump ring through the two upper 8⁰ seed beads in a Necklace Link. Before closing the jump ring, attach two 12-link chain pieces, and close the jump ring [**fig. 13**].

Crystal Connectors [fig. 14]

Thread a jump ring through the two upper 8⁰s on another Necklace Link, attach the available end of the chain in the previous Necklace Link and a 14-link chain piece, and close the jump ring. Thread a jump ring through the two lower 8⁰s under the chain just connected on the two Necklace Links. Before closing the jump ring, attach two Crystal Connectors, and close the jump ring. Attach the other end of each Crystal Connector to the lower jump ring of each Necklace Link using a ³⁄₁₆-in. jump ring. Continue to connect Necklace Links in this manner.

Final Assembly [fig. 15]

Attach a 14-link chain piece and a seven-link chain piece to each End Link and to half of the clasp as shown. Attach a Four-Loop Drop to the center Necklace Link using two jump rings. Use a ³⁄₁₆-in. jump ring and a ⅛-in. jump ring to attach each of the remaining Four-Loop Drops as shown.

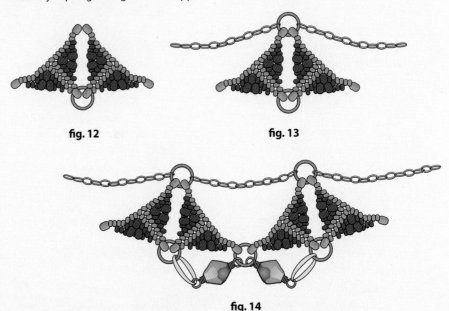

fig. 12

fig. 13

fig. 14

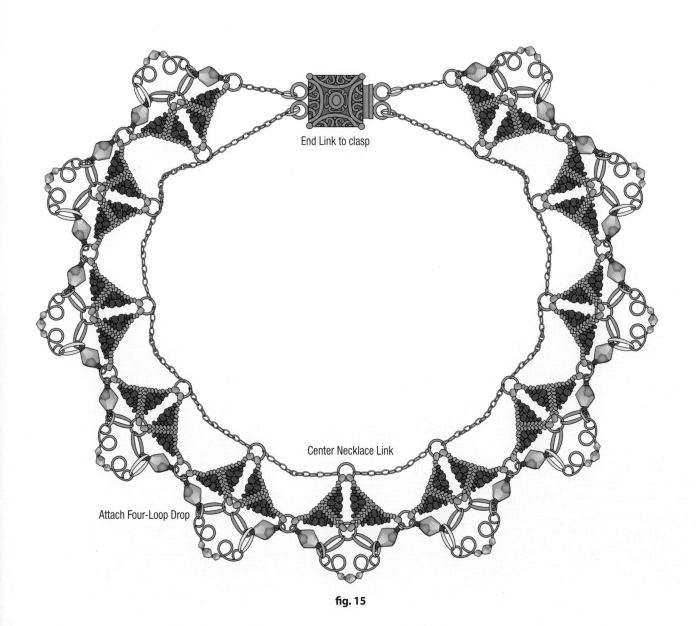

End Link to clasp

Center Necklace Link

Attach Four-Loop Drop

fig. 15

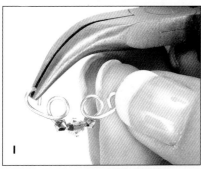

I

J

K

BRACELET

Setup

1 Make 28 Triangles following steps 1–10 of "Triangle." End the working threads. Keep the tail threads.

2 Make four Four-Loop Drops following steps 1–6 of "Four-Loop Drop," with the following alterations: Cut 2⅝ in. of wire instead of 2½ in. The extra ⅛ in. is needed to make a bigger end loop. The loop will be threaded through an 8º seed bead on an end link of the bracelet during assembly. Position the end of the wire in the second groove of the grooved looping pliers instead of the first groove when making the first loop.

Bracelet Link

Thread a needle on a tail of a Triangle. Sew through the next A 15º seed bead in the original ring of four beads. Pick up an 8mm crystal and another Triangle, and sew through two A 15ºs in the original ring of four beads opposite the two A 15ºs the tail is exiting in the Triangle just picked up. Sew back through the crystal and two A 15ºs in the original ring of four beads in the first Triangle, and end the tail [**fig. 16**]. Thread a needle on a tail of the opposite Triangle. Retrace the thread path, sewing through the opposite two A 15ºs in the original ring of four beads in both Triangles. End the tail thread. Create a total of 14 Bracelet Links.

Joined Bracelet Link

To make a Joined Bracelet Link, attach a ³⁄₁₆-in. jump ring through four 8ºs on two Bracelet Links as shown [**fig. 17**]. Join the remaining Bracelet Links in the same manner.

Assembly [fig. 18]

1 Attach Joined Bracelet Links using ⅛-in. and ³⁄₁₆-in. jump rings to assemble the bracelet band as shown. Using bentnose or chainnose pliers, open the larger first loop of a Four-Loop Drop by moving the loop away from you while holding the other end with your fingers [**J**]. Thread the left outer ring of the box end of the clasp onto the open loop of the Four-Loop Drop, and thread the open loop through the left center 8º in the End Link of the bracelet [**K**]. Make sure that the clasp ring is sitting inside the open loop of the Four-Loop Link.

2 Using pliers, close the loop. Flip over a second Four-Loop Drop and attach the larger first loop to the right center 8º in the End Link in the same manner. Using ³⁄₃₂-in.

jump rings, attach the outer loop of each Four-Loop Link to the outer jump rings on the End Link. Thread a ⅛-in. jump ring through the center ring of the box half of the clasp and the two inner loops of each Four-Loop Link, and close the jump ring.

3 Connect the slide half of the clasp to the other two Four-Loop Links and to the other End Link by attaching the larger first loop of each Four-Loop Link to the outer 8º in the End Link. Thread each outer ring of the slide between the loops of each Four-Loop Link as shown. Using ³⁄₃₂-in. jump rings, attach the inner loops of the Four-Loop Links to the ³⁄₁₆-in. jump ring on the End Link. Attach a ³⁄₁₆-in. jump ring between the inner loops of the Four-Loop Links and through the center ring of the slide half of the clasp.

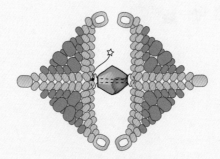

fig. 16

fig. 17

End Link to Four-Loop Drops to box clasp

Band assembly

End Link to Four-Loop Links to slide

fig. 18

fig. 19

EARRINGS

Setup

1 Make two Triangles following steps 1–10 of "Triangle." End both threads in Step 10.

2 Make two Four-Loop Drops following steps 1–6 of "Four-Loop Drop."

3 Make two Five-Loop Drops following steps 1 and 2 of "Five-Loop Drop."

Assembly [fig. 19]

Attach a Four-Loop Drop to a Triangle using two ⅛-in. jump rings. Attach a Five-Loop Drop to the Four-Loop Drop using two ³⁄₁₆-in. jump rings. Attach an earring finding to the Triangle using a ⅛-in. jump ring. Assemble a second earring.

Resources

This list of resources includes manufacturers and wholesale suppliers whose products may be available either at your local bead store, at a retail or wholesale trade show, or at an online retailer. I urge you to support your local bead store whenever possible for the materials and tools you need to make the designs in the book.

MATERIALS

COLORED FIRELINE
Sparkle Spot Bead Shop
727-424-4662
sparklespot.com

WIRE & JUMP RINGS
Red brass wire
Starr Gems, Inc.
800-882-8750
silversupplies.com

Titanium and bronze permanently colored copper wire
Paramount Wire Co. (Parawire)
973-672-0500
parawire.com

Parawire, red brass ³⁄₃₂ in. jump rings
Unkamen Supplies
unkamensupplies.etsy.com

Jump rings
C&T Designs, Inc.
855-2 MAILLE
candtdesigns.com

Closed jump rings
Fusion Beads, Inc.
888-781-3559
fusionbeads.com

FINDINGS
Bails and toggle clasps
TierraCast (wholesale only)
tierracast.com

Clasps
CGM Findings (wholesale only)
800-426-5246
cgmfindings.com

Claspgarten
claspgarten.com

Star's Clasps
starclaps.com

White Cloud Co.
718-830-3866

Earring findings with rhinestones
The Bead Smith
732-969-5300
helby.com (wholesale only)

Jill MacKay Collection
jillmackay.com and
Artbeads, artbeads.com

Patricia Healey fabricated copper
541-543-6613
patriciahealeycopper.com
(no products for sale on website)
Suppliers:
artbeads.com
limabeads.com
etsy.com/shop/bheartranch
panachegemsandbeads.com

CHAIN
Antique-silver-finish chain
Realm of the Goddess (wholesale only)
realmofthegoddess.com

Sterling silver textured oval chain
Kamal Trading Co.
714-236-0567
kamaltrading.com

BEADS
Drop beads
Caravan Beads
800-230-8941
caravanbeads.net

Teardrop beads (4x6mm)
John F. Allen & Son, Inc. (wholesale only)
jfallen.com
800-334-9971

Modebeads
modebeads.com
718-765-0124

Starman, Inc. (wholesale only)
360-683-3399
czechbeads.com

Top-drilled freshwater pearls
Fusion Beads Inc.
888-781-3559
fusionbeads.com

TOOLS

Bead On It Board
425-314-2077
beadonitboards.com

High-durability scissors for cutting Fireline
The Bead Smith
732-969-5300
helby.com (wholesale only)

Foldable 12-in. ruler
Student Supply (minimum purchase 12 rulers)
800-426-6351
studentsupply.com

Macaroni needle puller
Sharon Rawson
bdnrbonnet@aol.com

Wolf grooved looping pliers
Fusion Beads, Inc.
888-781-3559
fusionbeads.com

Wubbers pliers, pliers stand
Wired Up Beads
817-421-3030
wiredupbeads.com

SPECIALTY FINDINGS

This list will help you identify the manufacturers and wholesalers of some of the specialty findings I used in my designs. Please keep in mind that manufacturers regularly discontinue items. Your local bead store or supplier may be able to special-order an item or help you choose a good substitute.

BEGINNING
Rhythm & Blue Pearl
10x22mm sterling silver toggle clasp (White Cloud)
20x6mm rhodium-plated spring tongue three-row clasp (Claspgarten 13445/03-06-00-001)
Silver-plated earring findings with rhinestones (The Bead Smith)

Out of Idleness
15x12mm antique-copper-plated pewter two-loop clasp (TierraCast)

Wild Tile
10x18mm round hammered copper toggle clasp (Patricia Healey)
3mm oval copper-plated chain (Beads Galore CBS 285)

Count Your Blossoms
Gold-plated spring tongue three-row clasp
   (Claspgarten 13075/03)
Gold-plated earring findings with rhinestones
   (The Bead Smith)

BROADENING
Gibsonia Girl
3mm oval antique-silver-finish chain (Realm of
   the Goddess, Venus-1)
35x13mm sterling silver or stainless steel Oval
   Floral Connectors (Jill MacKay JM012)
Antique-silver-plated pewter leaf hook-and-eye
   clasp (TierraCast)
Sterling silver Triple Strand Twig Bead Spacer
   (Jill MacKay SPC001)
10mm silver-plated rose magnetic clasp
   (Jill MacKay JMC1046)

Modern Vintage
10mm stainless steel Openwork bead
   (Jill MacKay JMSSB028 S)
4x8mm stainless steel Saucer Spacer
   (Jill MacKay JMSSB022 S)
2mm sterling silver textured oval chain
   (Kamal Trading Co., SS-TC25-7)
9x10mm antique-silver-plated pewter vine
   prong bail (TierraCast)
23x19mm antique-silver-plated oval toggle
   clasp (Jill MacKay JMC1040)
12.5mm antique-silver-plated pewter classic
   toggle clasp (TierraCast)

Growing Frida's Flower
Small green stone-finish teardrop
   (Artbeads)
Hammered copper square toggle clasp
   (Patricia Healey)

BUILDING
In Buttons and Bowls
Hammered copper toggle clasp (Patricia Healey)

A Star Is Born
Sterling silver toggle clasp (White Cloud)

A Piece of the Past
2mm textured 14k gold oval chain
   (Kamal Trading Co., TC22-14)
Vermeil 2-strand filigree box clasp (Star's Clasps)
Gold-filled 3-strand filigree box clasp
   (CGM findings)

Acknowledgments

I would like to thank my husband, Jason, for taking the photographs of the materials, tools, and step-by-step processes for the book. Along with his photographic skills, his invaluable contributions of love and patience made this book possible. Thank you, Met Innmon, for spending many hours as my unofficial and unpaid first-line technical editor. Thank you, Nancy Cain, for helping me improve the content at various stages. Thank you, Mary Wohlgemuth, my editor at Kalmbach, for educating me about the publishing process and guiding me through it with the patience of a true professional. Thanks also go to the rest of the Kalmbach team—Bill Zuback, who gave Jason and me expert direction for our process photography, and James Forbes, for the beautiful lead photos; Lisa Bergman and Lisa Schroeder, who created a lovely design and layouts. Thank you, Chrisa West, for your enthusiasm for all things—including wireworking. And finally, a special thanks to my fellow travelers on a creative journey who purchased this book along the way.

About the Author

Teresa Meister has enjoyed making art for as long as she can remember, playing with many different media from finger paint to pastels to photography. She had a "Eureka!" moment the day her eyes landed on a rainbow-hued wall of seed beads in a craft store more than 20 years ago.

Today beads are at the heart of her jewelry designs, and she loves finding new ways to use seed beads to communicate her ideas. In recent years, she has incorporated beadweaving with fine wirework to create jewelry with a distinctive, graceful look.

Teresa holds a bachelor of fine arts degree from Mason Gross School of the Arts, Rutgers University. Teresa was profiled in the German beading magazine *Perlen Poesie* (Issue #6) and has contributed to *Bead Unique* and other beading magazines. She teaches her designs nationally. Teresa lives in the beautiful Rocky Mountain foothills with her husband of more than 25 years, Jason, and their two beloved greyhounds, Bob and Ray.

Connect to more creative stitching projects!

Artistic Seed Bead Jewelry

Discover how to transform your inspirational sources into gorgeous jewelry as you work through 13 beautiful, bead-stitched designs. You'll learn tips for choosing bead colors and finishes, how to "audition" your beads, and which stitch to use to achieve your desired effect.

64292 • $21.95

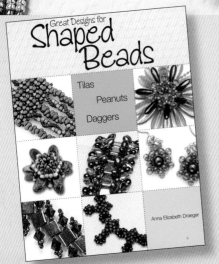

Contemporary Cube Bead Designs

Stitch these delightful bead shapes into 28 striking projects, from bold cuffs to multistrand rope necklaces to elegant earrings. Step-by-step-instructions, detailed illustrations, and tons of expert tips will help bead stitchers with some experience show everyone it's hip to be square!

64360 • $19.95

Great Designs for Shaped Beads

Tilas, daggers, peanuts, drops — learn how to show them off to their best advantage! Popular designer Anna Elizabeth Draeger guides you through 24 stitching projects for earrings, necklaces, rings, and bracelets, each with dazzling design alternatives. You'll enjoy 50+ creative ideas in all!

64957 • $19.95